Leslie
from Hannah
Dec. 2014

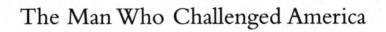
The Man Who Challenged America

The Man Who Challenged America

The Life and Obsession of Sir Thomas Lipton

LAURENCE BRADY

BIRLINN

First published in 2007 by
Birlinn Limited
West Newington House
10 Newington Road
Edinburgh
EH9 1QS

www.birlinn.co.uk

ISBN13: 978 1 84158 578 9
ISBN10: 1 84158 578 5

British Library Cataloguing-in-Publication Data
A catalogue record for this book is available from the British Library

Design and typeset by Textype, Cambridge
Printed and bound by Creative Print and Design, Wales

For Celia

Contents

List of Illustrations

Acknowledgements

Sir Thomas Lipton is a compelling figure: an innovative and audacious entrepreneur; a business leader whose sense of corporate responsibility to his employees, customers and the communities he served was second nature; an unofficial diplomat trusted by kings and presidents; and a man whose passion for one of the greatest trophies in sport won over even his most vocal critics.

But the Scottish journalist and author Bob Crampsey was absolutely right when he noted that Sir Thomas presents a problem for a biographer. He left behind no family, no diaries and no personal correspondence. In *The Man Who Challenged America* I have endeavoured to remain true to the facts as I discovered them and, where appropriate, to question some of Sir Thomas's more dubious assertions – he had an enviable gift for storytelling and at times it has been a challenge to separate fact from fiction.

In researching this book I have made extensive use of Glasgow's

Mitchell Library archive of Lipton press volumes and I would like to thank Dr O'Brien and her colleagues there for their courtesy and helpfulness. I would also like to acknowledge support in my research from Louisa Watrous of the Mystic Seaport Museum in Connecticut; Tess Bogar and Michael Levitt of the New York Yacht Club; Dr Andrew Alexander of the University of Surrey; Jeannette Strickland and her colleagues at the Unilever Archive; the staff at the British Library, the Scottish Screen Archive, the New York Public Library, the Scottish Maritime Museum in Dumbarton and the National Maritime Museum; Mark O'Neill and Rosemary Watt of Glasgow Museums; Lyn Ford of Shrewsbury Museums; Dr John Blow and Menna Rees of the Sir Thomas Lipton Memorial Home for Nurses, Osidge; Monsignor Leo Cushley; Dr Mary McHugh, archivist of the Archdiocese of Glasgow; Father Edmund Highton; May Fife Kohn; David Williamson of Matthew Algie & Sons; Ian Fraser; and Jane Reilly of Globe Pequot Press.

I would also like to thank the America's Cup insiders without whose co-operation, generosity and knowledge I could not have written this biography. I am particularly indebted to Bob Fisher, sailing correspondent for *The Guardian* and *The Observer* and America's Cup historian, who opened many doors, and whose love of the America's Cup is infectious. I am also very grateful to Marcus Hutchinson, director of America's Cup Media Relations; Bruno Troublé, a former America's Cup skipper and adviser to Louis Vuitton; Ed Gorman of *The Times*; and Peter Lester, a former America's Cup-winning sailor with Sir Peter Blake.

At various stages of my three-year journey in writing *The Man Who Challenged America* I have received tremendous goodwill and encouragement from a number of individuals. In particular I would like to thank Kenny Kemp and Alan Cunningham who have given so much helpful advice and support. I would also like to acknowledge the kindness of Nigel Macdonald, Professor Ian Percy, Lord Robertson of Port Ellen, Philip Downie of the Royal Ulster Yacht Club and Mark Stanton of Jenny Brown Associates. To Hugh Andrew, Andrew Simmons, Aline Hill, Sarah Ream, Peter Burns and all of the team at Birlinn, I offer my sincere thanks for their enthusiasm for the book, their guidance and wisdom.

In the writing of this biography, the love, example and inspiration of my mum and dad have never been far from my mind. My wife Celia and my children Anne, Sarah and Jonathan have also played key roles in the process, allowing me the time and solitude necessary to write. I am so grateful to them for their understanding and patience. My brother Brendan, sisters Monica and Clare and my wider family and friends have, in different ways, also been helpful and supportive – thanks to all.

Finally, I confess to being a latecomer to the skill and thrill of the America's Cup. In Britain at least it is still greatly undervalued as an international sporting event, but I hope that the British challenge – renewed for the thirty-third America's Cup – will help stimulate a new passion for what is often described as the oldest trophy in sport.

Laurence Brady
April 2007

Preface

I wish I was a big man and could build the fastest yacht in the world. I would give it to Sir Tommy as my papa says he is the greatest, grandest and most gallant sportsman in the big world.

– Eleven-year-old schoolboy from Boston, 1903

A sportsman? Hardly. Thomas Lipton (1850–1931), the grocer from Glasgow who rose from relative poverty to create a global business brand wasn't even a sailor. He certainly wasn't a Victorian Alan Bond, Larry Ellison or Ted Turner – all wealthy businessmen who converted their own love of sailing into multimillion-dollar campaigns for yachting's greatest prize, the America's Cup. Unlike them, Tommy never took the helm; he didn't know his spinnaker from his spars and he knew nothing of gybing or tacking. Yet despite this, the schoolboy from Boston is not mistaken. In Tommy's attitudes towards his opponents and towards defeat he was indeed a great sportsman, in the true sense of the word, and it is more than fitting that he is honoured in the America's Cup Hall of Fame.

In fact, if the trend for making lists and virtual halls of fame continues, then Thomas Lipton deserves to make more than one appearance. He could also feature in a businessman-turned-diplomat 'top ten'. His record in corporate responsibility was impressive, and in his employee relations he was almost peerless. Certainly, too, he merits a place as one of the great business innovators, having played no small role in revolutionising the grocery business in Britain. Then, of course, there's the list of the most enduring brands of all time. Within Tommy's own lifetime, Lipton's Tea transformed the drinking habits of at least one nation. Even in Britain, where the Lipton brand is not as ubiquitous as it is in other parts of the world, there is still an understanding that if you're talking about Lipton you must be talking about tea. In fact the Lipton brand, now owned by Unilever, is one of the top five beverage brands in the world today, measured by consumption. There is now even Pepsi Lipton International, a joint venture between Unilever and Pepsico that capitalises on the global ready-to-drink tea markets.

And – not that anyone would ever be mad enough to create such a list – Tommy Lipton could lay legitimate claim to being the most Irish American Scot of all time. Though Tommy was born in the Gorbals district of Glasgow, Scotland's second city, and once the second city of the British Empire, his parents came from Ulster. All of his family was born in Ireland, and he retained a deep sense of his Irish heritage and character throughout his life. Every one of his America's Cup challengers was named 'Shamrock' and he represented the Royal Ulster Yacht Club in those challenges. It is no wonder, then, that he was frequently referred to as Irish in the American media. As for his life-long love affair with America, this was shaped by his first visit there in his teenage years. The contrast between what he had experienced at home and the American approach to life and business was so stark that it changed his entire outlook.

If there are two other fascinations which equal the modern popular obsession with making lists, they are celebrity and sports. Thomas Lipton was unquestionably and beyond all doubt one of the best-known and, it might be added, best-loved public figures in the world from the late 1890s to his death in 1931. Unlike today's celebrities, however, he was spared intrusions into his private life: the media accepted what he told them and no journalist probed too deeply into his past. For his part, he chose not to wear his heart on his sleeve in the most private of matters and carefully constructed the Lipton image through the preservation of press articles and interviews.

As for being a winner in sport, Tommy Lipton accumulated a Michael Schumacher-sized collection of trophies and awards for yachting. Yet cynics might argue that he is like a Brazilian football manager who never won a World Cup, or a golfer or tennis player who topped the earnings list but never won a major title. Tommy was indeed often pigeonholed as the world's greatest loser. It might actually be said that he made an art of losing, even rendering the victor's win almost unimportant, because in every contest the public and the press, whether in Britain or America or anywhere else, only really wanted to talk about Lipton. Tommy would have been the first to deny this: there was nothing he wanted more in the last thirty years of his life than to win the America's Cup for the Royal Ulster Yacht Club and Britain. It was his dream to be remembered as the man who challenged America and won, as the man who brought back the America's Cup to Britain, not as the world's best loser or even 'Tea Tom'. It was definitely not by design but is nevertheless true that Tommy was famed and revered for his gold medal performances in sportsmanship every time he stepped into the public arena. The reactions to his defeats in America and the outpouring of affection for him over thirty years were truly remarkable: imagine the American public willing the Europeans to win the Ryder Cup or cheering on the Russians against the USA in an Olympic ice hockey match.

Without a doubt, Tommy Lipton's name ought to appear on any list of the 'greatest, grandest and most gallant sportsmen in the big world'.

1

Columbia, the first challenge, 1899

Throughout the spring of 1899 the whole of America was eagerly awaiting the return of a national hero. The man in question was Admiral George Dewey, commander of the US Navy's Asiatic Squadron whose victory at Manila Bay on 1 May 1898 was the first major engagement of the Spanish–American war – a short-lived conflict which ended in a decisive American victory three months later. Across the country, millions of people followed Dewey's progress in the newspapers as he made his way back via Ceylon, Gibraltar, Trieste, Naples and Villefranche towards an ecstatic welcome. In the event, however, his homecoming did not quite work out as planned. Early on a summer's morning in 1899, the *Olympia*, the cruiser onboard which Dewey had led the small squadron of American ships into Manila Bay the year before, gently steamed into New York Harbour several days before she was expected. Though this was the moment America had been anticipating for months, she was caught napping. But who should be awake and alive to this discovery? Sir Thomas Lipton, on board his private yacht in readiness for his forthcoming challenge for the America's Cup, arguably the world's greatest maritime prize.

With an entrepreneur's presence of mind, Tommy quickly summoned what newspapermen he could find at such an early hour and set off on his own launch for the *Olympia*. Welcomed aboard, he was taken to meet the admiral in his cabin and breakfast with him. Tommy noted, 'Admiral Dewey was tremendously interested in the forthcoming races and we had a lot to talk about.' As Tommy departed an hour later *Olympia*'s crew were lining the rails, waving their tea packets at him. 'At first I was non-plussed at these packages. Then I suddenly remembered that some weeks previously the *Olympia* had called in at Ceylon on her way home from the Philippines, and that I had cabled instructions to my manager out there to present every man of the crew with a package of Lipton's tea. These packages were now on their way home to the sailors' wives and sweethearts.' Needless to say, all of these events were reported upon extensively. Tommy was quick to capitalise still further on this unexpected coup by inviting Dewey and his senior officers aboard his own yacht, *Erin*, that same evening, in order to reciprocate the admiral's hospitality. Dewey could only accept the offer.

In no small measure, Americans – politicians, press and the public alike – applauded Tommy's style and self-confidence. There was definitely something different about this man, and he certainly wasn't the staid, imperialist, patronising aristocrat many had come to expect from Britain. Almost overnight, Tommy gained both acceptance and respect in America in a way that had been unimaginable only days before. He was rewarded with the honour of *Erin* leading the port column in the triumphant parade of ships in celebration of Dewey's return.

However, even when the parade was over, Tommy wasn't quite able to focus on his main purpose for being in New York, namely his challenge to win the America's Cup. Two days after the city of New York ground to a halt for the naval reception and street parade, he was invited to a dinner at the Waldorf Hotel with the ratings and the petty officers of the *Olympia*. As Bob Crampsey noted in his book on Lipton, Tommy was fascinated by the idea of these men at the bottom of the naval ladder being entertained in one of New York's most prestigious hotels: 'It was difficult to imagine a couple of ship's companies taking over Claridge's or the Savoy.'

As with so many other key points in his life, Tommy gives no true indication of his feelings or his mental strength as he approached his first challenge for the America's Cup. Yet, in that long celebratory weekend that preceded the first of the races, due to take place on the Tuesday, Tommy was surely elated by his masterful timing. He had first thought about the cup twelve years previously and had written to the MP for Cork, WJ Lynn, offering to put up the money for an all-Irish challenger – that is, a boat built in Ireland and crewed exclusively by the Irish. It had proved impossible, however, as there simply wasn't the boat-building or sailing expertise in Ireland at that time. However, quite apart from the extremely fortuitous arrival of the victorious Dewey, there are three reasons why Tommy's 1899 challenge was far better timed than anything considered in the late 1880s.

Firstly, Tommy had absolutely no public profile outside of the grocery business in 1887. By contrast, in 1899 he was known across Britain, having been knighted the previous year. Secondly, his business life consumed him in the 1880s; he was still mentally a hundred miles away from creating time for another pursuit, and, not having even been close to yacht racing or even sailing per se, he had no idea of the commitment, in terms of time and money, that an America's Cup challenge entailed.

Thirdly, on the international stage, relations between the countries had recently soured, with America taking a very dim view of what it perceived to be an unsavoury blend of British greed and aggression in South Africa's Transvaal, where the occupying Boers wanted to protect their land and newly found gold. By 1899 war looked inevitable, and American sympathy, by and large, lay with the Boers; *The New York Times* referred to the British position as 'very sad and very shameful'. Though this may sound like bad timing, in fact it represented an opportunity to heal relations and show Americans a different side of Britishness.

Even though American industrial might had gained such power and momentum and Britain's status as the first industrialised nation had lost its lustre, the America's Cup aroused strong emotions on both sides of the Atlantic – so strong, in fact, that all the rational economic, and at times diplomatic, certainties of nationhood were left behind. To understand exactly why this sailing contest – for that's what it was, one yacht racing another – assumed such national importance, and just why Tommy Lipton was the right man at the right time to challenge for it in 1899, requires some understanding of the cup's genesis.

In 1851, when Tommy was just a baby, the British home of yacht racing was, then as now, at Cowes on the Isle of Wight under the auspices of the Royal Yacht Squadron. Founded as the Yacht Club in 1815, in the aftermath of Waterloo, the squadron's members were given the unique privilege of being allowed to fly the white naval ensign by the Admiralty in 1829. Royal status was granted by King William IV in 1833. In short, the Royal Yacht Squadron at Cowes was ordained as the premier yachting arena in Britain and, by extension, the world, given Britain's reputation for producing the best sailors and the best boats.

Though there was no formal challenge to the rest of the world to come and beat the best of British yachts, there had been some bragging and isolated yachting duels in previous years. The very idea of a yacht purpose-built in America being strong enough to withstand the pounding of an Atlantic crossing but still fast enough to beat the best of British yachts on her arrival would have seemed preposterous in 1850. Even if the yacht in question had the talismanic name *America*, cost $20,000 and embodied all the technology and sailing know-how that the New World had to offer, and even if she didn't have the old-fashioned cod's head and mackerel tail design, but was broad and shallow with a long, hollow bow and fine-cut sails, her sailors wouldn't know the wind conditions in the Solent half as well as British yachtsmen. Anyway, the following year Britain planned to showcase her supremacy to the world in the Great Exhibition; the Americans surely wouldn't choose that moment for a blatantly foolhardy challenge.

Yet that's just what they did. The idea – unexpected and financially and reputationally risky as it was – belonged to John Stevens, a New York business man who owed his own success and wealth in no small measure to the innovations and entrepreneurial spirit of his father, Colonel John Stevens. Colonel Stevens had set his son an example by building his reputation and his wealth on achieving a number of firsts: his was the first steam ferry to cross the Hudson as a service, and he ran the first ferry service to Philadelphia.

Stevens Junior built, sailed and raced boats in New York's harbour. It was on one of these, the schooner *Gimcrack*, that he decided to form the New York Yacht Club with eight of his friends. Stevens thus achieved his own first: becoming the first commodore of the New York Yacht Club. From this foundation, the idea to build *America* was born. He formed a syndicate of five friends to spread the financial risk. Even so, he was still in danger of ridiculing his family's business reputation at home and his country's standing – not just in sailing – abroad. Yet these factors were heavily outweighed by youthful confidence, an entrepreneurial conviction that a challenge could be met and overcome and a simple nationalistic belief that America was not inferior to Britain. *America* would not be second-rate.

So, *America* crossed the Atlantic. The Royal Yacht Squadron offered every courtesy and facility, but Stevens threw down the gauntlet, suggesting a race between *America* and any Royal Yacht Squadron yacht over 20 to 70 miles for a prize of £10,000. There was no direct answer, but teased by *The Times* about British dedication to 'our national naval spirit', the Royal Yacht Squadron made a counter proposition, inviting the *America* to participate in a challenge cup valued at £100.

On 22 August 1851, with Queen Victoria watching aboard the royal yacht *Victoria and Albert*, *America* triumphed. Luck only played a small part in her victory. The yacht's design, especially her elegant bow, combined with fine seamanship and her well-cut cotton sails, contributed to a well-deserved victory. Within a month of this puncturing of British naval pride, Commodore Stevens and his syndicate made a handsome profit by selling *America* for $25,000 to the Irish peer Lord John de Blaquière. With hindsight, it is hard to fathom why they denied themselves not only the public adulation, affection and gratitude that would have greeted them when they sailed back into New York Harbour, but also the much greater business opportunities that *America*'s physical presence could have created.

Stevens himself was to die only six years later. The cup itself had originally and erroneously been known in the New York papers as the Queen's Cup, but it was soon renamed after the yacht that had won it. So, with Stevens's passing, the America's Cup and its accompanying Deed of Gift became the property of the New York Yacht Club. This Deed of Gift established that the cup would be a perpetual challenge 'for friendly competition between foreign countries'. The challenging yacht club would need to reach agreement with the defending club about the terms of racing. The challenging club was also obliged to give six months' notice.

They may have failed to capitalise on the great commercial opportunity of *America*, but what tremendous foresight Stevens and his friends showed in immortalising their achievement. The America's Cup was born. The fact that the Americans competed at Cowes in 1853 with a schooner, *Sylvie*, reputedly faster than *America*, and were soundly beaten by an English cutter, *Julia*, somehow didn't matter. It couldn't undo the damage done two years previously. Britain's dominant position as ruler of the waves had been exposed as a myth. The British would have to take back the trophy that symbolised a nation's seamanship. They would have to win the America's Cup.

Initially, challenges were slow in coming, with the American Civil War and its aftermath delaying the feasibility of matches taking place. However, from 1870 onwards they came fast and furious. Each time, they were successfully rebuffed by the defending craft of the New York Yacht Club. The first few challenges emanated from Britain, predictably enough. Not so predictably, however, they were put together by James Ashbury, an ambitious entrepreneur who was not recognised as a member of the more established British yachting classes. In 1881 the Bay of Quinte Yacht Club of Belleville, Ontario, Canada raced the untried challenger *Atlanta* unsuccessfully in a match against the immeasurably better equipped and sailed *Mischief*.

More British challenges were to follow, in 1885, 1886 and 1887 respectively. Two of these emanated from Scotland: first, the *Galatea*, representing the Royal Northern Yacht Club and secondly, *Thistle*, flying the flag of the Royal Clyde Yacht Club. On each occasion, both failed to win a single match in the best of five series, though the Scots were not without some fine sailors and designers.

These challenges witnessed the New York Yacht Club's assertion of its authority over the rules of engagement and, to some degree, the dilution of the essence of the cup as a friendly competition between foreign countries as represented by yacht clubs. However, the minor altercations that had arisen were as nothing compared to the America's Cup storm that would rage in the 1890s. It was this next chapter in America's Cup history that rendered Tommy Lipton's arrival and conduct in 1899 so astonishing. But in this early period of the America's Cup, from 1871 to the mid 1890s, Tommy was, quite literally, minding his own business. He had nothing to do with either of the Scottish challenges, and the idea of him, a Glasgow grocer, being linked in any way to the Royal Yacht Squadron was inconceivable.

Histories of the America's Cup have not been kind to Windham Thomas Wyndham-Quin, 4th Earl of Dunraven and three times challenger for the America's Cup. Inauspiciously, in 1889 his first challenger, *Valkyrie*, never even raised a sail in an America's Cup match. The Royal Yacht Squadron, in whose name he challenged, would not agree to a new New York Yacht Club Deed of Gift ruling in which challengers were required to divulge additional dimensions and not just the length of their boat at the waterline.

Dunraven, a stranger to tact and diplomacy who seemed to embody the worst of the British Establishment, withdrew, but he persisted in hectoring the New York Yacht Club with his views on match conditions. The niggling continued until the club accepted a new challenger, *Valkyrie II*, whose waterline length only would be known to the defender. Even so, *Valkyrie II* was soundly beaten by *Vigilant*, the first America's Cup yacht designed by Nathanael Greene Herreshoff, a man whose genius was acknowledged even by Lord Dunraven.

Dunraven's third challenger was inevitably named *Valkyrie III*. The 1895 defender, helpfully christened *Defender*, was another Herreshoff design and was skippered by Hank Haff, who had already tasted America's Cup glory on *Volunteer* in 1887. If that wasn't enough to unsettle Dunraven, the volume of excursionists and spectator craft lining the course undoubtedly was, not least because his own *Valkyrie II* had been sunk after a collision during a race on the River Clyde the previous year, resulting in the loss of one life. As Lord Dunraven later recalled, he felt it was his 'duty' to protest against the poor policing of the racecourse. He also complained that *Defender* had added extra ballast before the first race, but this accusation was rejected.

After an emphatic defeat in the first race *Valkyrie III* led *Defender* home by a clear 47 seconds in the second race, but she was disqualified for damaging her opponent's deck and topmast shroud with her boom – though not deliberately – at the start of the match. *Valkyrie III* did not complete the third race in protest at interference from other vessels on the course. Worse still, Dunraven returned home and, at this safe distance, wrote a stinging rebuke of the New York Yacht Club and her managing owner Charles Oliver Iselin in a magazine article. In essence, he alleged that victory had been achieved by illegitimate means. Dunraven was quickly struck off as a member of the New York Yacht Club.

Dunraven was not, in fact, without backbone and compassion. If not courageous, he certainly had a spirit of adventure. A one-time war correspondent for the *Daily Telegraph*, he had witnessed the 1870 war between France and Prussia. He was also partial to big-game shooting and spent time hunting in the United States with none other than Buffalo Bill. He was also a successful yachtsman in his own right over many years, winning, for example, the King's Cup at Cowes in 1912 in his cruising ketch, *Cariad II*. He cared about the morale of his crew, and in 1895, the same year as the contentious challenge, he was elected a London county councillor for the borough of Wandsworth on the basis of his concern for working-class housing in the area.

Sadly, though, Thomas Wyndham-Quin, 4th Earl of Dunraven, is remembered for insensitivity. Single-handedly, he generated an enormous amount of ill-feeling between two friendly nations. At a time when the America's Cup was the sporting contest of the age, his actions made front-page news. An estimated 65,000 spectators had watched *Valkyrie III* and *Defender* race, and the resentment of being accused of unfair play was keenly felt across the United States. So potent was the mix of national pride, prestige, sailing prowess and technological mastery vested in the America's Cup by 1895 that his actions brought Anglo-American relations to a new low. In his autobiography he expressed no regrets but still felt a sense of shock years afterwards about 'an amount of excitement that could not have been exceeded if someone had deliberately hurled an insult at the American nation. The tide of feeling ran very high.'

By 1899 Tommy Lipton was a national figure in Britain, a flamboyant and generous millionaire businessman whose profile was instantly recognised in any main street from Aberdeen to Brighton. Now in his late forties, he was balding, perhaps somewhat prematurely. His jolly, ruddy complexion was complimented by piercing blue eyes and a long, straight nose, but masked by a moustache of truly obscene dimensions. Standing tall at 5 feet 11 inches, he dressed smartly in finely cut, textured clothing. More often than not he sported a subtle cravat over a starched white shirt, but he was no dandy and was not given to posturing.

During his near thirty years of business he had worked hard at developing his own style and persona. Tommy presented himself as a hard-working man of the people, a showman even, who had made the drudgery and hardship of purchasing the necessities of life, such as eggs, ham and tea, both a pleasurable and an affordable experience. His way of life was about serving other people, giving customers what they wanted. He was an entrepreneur with a keen sense of responsibility to his employees and the thousands of ordinary people who chose Lipton's because he kept his prices within their reach. He oozed charm in a smooth blend of Irish-Scottishness. He possessed that rare gift of putting whomever he was addressing – whether the poorest of his cus-tomers, his own staff or VIPs – immediately at their ease. No airs and graces, he was just Tommy Lipton, on a mission, it would seem, to dis-arm everyone in his path.

In short, his style and presentation were about as far removed as it was possible to be from Lord Dunraven and the members of the Royal Yacht Squadron, though he was no less passionate about being British and loyal to the British Crown. If anything, his recently acquired sta-tus as knight of the realm and friend of the Prince of Wales, not to mention the successful flotation of his company, had confirmed his belief that his cultivated, courteous open-handed style could work wonders for all that he held dear – for queen and country, for the

Prince of Wales, who loved yachting, for Lipton's and for the great mass of ordinary working-class British people who deserved a far better representative than the likes of Dunraven. He would be a people's champion, a man who could put an end to the embarrassment and show the Americans what the British were really like.

Even overlooking the fact that he first considered an America's Cup challenge in the 1880s, it seems rather disingenuous of Tommy that in the first mention on yachting in his autobiography *Leaves from the Lipton Log* (1931) he frames his interest in the cup as a return to his boyhood passion for sailing, by which he really means the thrill of being at sea on a yacht: 'it was not until the year 1898 that I found my thoughts definitely and longingly turning again to my boyhood passion — to the wind and the waves and the salt spray lashing and a mast bending under a well-filled sail'. He claims that his intent in entering the cup was to gratify his 'zest for the sea and give [him] more frequent respites from the cares of business. The appeal was almost irresistible.' As so often with Tommy Lipton, this was only half of the truth.

Just one of the facts that he doesn't mention is that his America's Cup challenger was called *Shamrock*. This was not merely in deference to his Irish heritage or in homage to his model sailing boat of his youth in Glasgow: it was also a shrewd nod to a growing American market, a market that had more readily embraced the charm and vitality of many of its Irish immigrants than the arguably more serious-minded and less tolerant Scots. He chose, too, to mount his challenge through the Royal Ulster Yacht Club, demonstrating that he was not part of the landed British Establishment and honouring his parents' birthplace. Moreover, although much of *Shamrock I* was fabricated on mainland Britain, her rigging was fitted at the Harland & Wolf shipyard in Belfast, and her masts were also furnished in Ireland.

The crew, however, was a mixture of English and Scottish sailors. *Shamrock I*'s skipper was also a Scot, Captain Archie Hogarth. Hogarth came from a traditional seafaring family and his father was well known the length of the Firth of Clyde. Hogarth owed his reputation as the best available skipper to his adept handling of the yacht *Isolde* over several seasons. He had also skippered the racing yacht *Calluna*, designed by William Fife, designer of Lord Dunraven's *Valkyrie II*. Hogarth was assisted by Captain Robert Wringe. Wringe was hired because he was from Brightlingsea in Essex. He therefore had a good understanding of the majority of the crew, who came from the Colne-side villages of Wivenhoe and Rowehedge as well as Brightlingsea.

Shamrock I herself was another William Fife design, built by Thornycroft & Co. near London. She was 89 feet on the waterline and constructed with steel frames and manganese bronze plating. However, delays in her construction allowed only the briefest of racing trials to take place in British waters: just one completed race, over a 40-mile stretch off the coast at Southampton against the Prince of Wales' race-winner, *Britannia*, which had previously performed well against both *Vigilant* and *Valkyrie*. *Shamrock I* won handsomely, defeating *Britannia* with more than 16 minutes to spare. The omens were good. Tommy crowed, 'After the trial races this week both Mr Fife and I were convinced that *Shamrock* is a magnificent vessel. She is the fastest ever seen on this side of the ocean . . . Of course I cannot say how the *Shamrock* compares with the *Columbia* . . . but we are satisfied that we have a game boat and . . . we expect to make at least a good showing.' A second trial with *Britannia* was cut short when the Prince of Wales, who was on board, had to leave for another appointment.

Shamrock I was towed by Tommy's own yacht, *Erin*, up to Greenock on the west coast of Scotland in July 1899. Here her hull was

17

strengthened and heavy planks laid on her deck in preparation for her transatlantic voyage. Tommy was optimistic, though in truth the trials were almost useless as a meaningful test of her speed and handling. Tellingly, the following tale of *Shamrock I* was recounted by a *New York Herald* correspondent a few days before her launch. 'On my way from Glasgow two shipbuilders got into the same apartment with me. After asking the usual questions one said, "I never saw anything like that mast and those spars. They are out of all proportion to the hull." After I reached Greenock I heard the same remark on all sides.'

It took *Shamrock I* fifteen days to cross the Atlantic, arriving in New York's harbour on 18 August. She had until 3 October to be ready for *Columbia*. In this period Tommy found himself having to defend the challenger's chances against the growing weight of opinion in *Columbia*'s favour amongst experienced yachtsmen. One such was Clinton Crane, the respected New York yacht designer. Crane declared, '*Shamrock* has apparently a hard bilge, a flat floor and greater beam than the *Columbia* and thus should be more powerful. She must also have a greater wetted surface than the Herreshoff boat and consequently should be slower in lighter airs and moderate weather generally . . . it is my opinion the Cup will stay with us a while longer'. Captain Henry Hoffman, the last surviving member of the *America* concurred: 'Our boat is built for fair weather while *Shamrock* is a heavy weather boat. In light winds the Herreshoff yacht will run away from the British craft. Even when the seas run high . . . *Columbia* will not be at a disadvantage. She may not be able to carry as much canvas, but her easier lines will enable her to plough through heavy seas with shortened sails just as fast if not faster than *Shamrock*.' Tommy, however, would have been pleased to hear of his friend Andrew Carnegie's comments when asked about the challenge: 'One thing I know, that is, there were many of the best American sportsmen who would have been pleased if *Valkyrie* won the last race. There will be more this time who will wish, in the interests of international sport, that the *Shamrock* will take back the trophy. The feeling is pretty general that the Cup has remained long enough on one side.'

Tommy, for his part, proved his own skill in parrying media questions, this time about the readiness of *Shamrock I*. Unfailingly, he complimented the New York Yacht Club and the hospitality he had received in the United States. As for the challenger, 'You see, I do not skipper the yacht and did not make her sails. Fife did the designing and Ratsey made the sails, so they know more on these subjects than I do. But the whole point now is that the best boat shall win.'

As cynics would have it, the whole point was that Lipton was in this for the promotion of his business. He wasn't a yachtsman, and he had no track record in the sport. He had yet to learn the language of yacht racing, to understand that yachts couldn't sail directly into the wind and to see that sailors viewed the race zone as a slope, with the wind blowing from the top back to the bottom, where the start line was located. The first leg of the race was always sailed into the wind, so it was 'upwind', 'windward' or even 'on the beat'. On the windward leg to the marker at the top of the course, the boat's mainsail and its headsail, called either a genoa or a jib, had to be sheeted in tight. This meant, as Sir Thomas Lipton was yet to learn, that both sails had to be as close to the centre of the yacht as possible, or 'close-hauled' as it was known.

To reach this windward mark the competing yachts had to take a zigzag route, and this, as Sir Thomas would soon know well enough, was called tacking. After rounding the mark, with the wind now behind them, each yacht would throw up a huge three-cornered lightweight sail known as the spinnaker. This sailing downwind was called sailing to leeward. Zigzagging on this leeward leg, the changing of direction within a 180-degree angle, was not called tacking, but gybing. If the race committee determined that the course on any given day was to be triangular, with a final leg that was neither windward nor leeward, the yachts would be 'reaching', or sailing across the wind, to the finish.

But did it really matter that Tommy had no personal racing experience of beating to windward or leaning out on the windward rail with the rest of the crew to balance a yacht as she scythed through the waves? Tommy certainly didn't think so and, if anything, hinted at brilliance of design as being the deciding factor. He told reporters before leaving England, 'No possible outlay has been spared to make *Shamrock* the better boat. I have done my best. With the highest evidence obtainable I have devoted all possible time and thought to perfecting every detail. The financial consideration has been ignored and whatever money could do has been done. I believe the Herreshoffs to be, without question, the finest boat designers in the world . . . and so it does not follow we are certain to win.'

This ignoring of the 'financial consideration' also included providing incentives for victory: £100 for Captain Hogarth, £50 for Captain Wringe, £40 for the mate and £28 each for the crew. Given that *Shamrock I* had a full complement of sixty-six men this was not an insubstantial offer. In total, Tommy had spent approximately £140,000 on *Shamrock I*, £40,000 more than he originally intended, and certainly more than the banker JP Morgan's syndicate had expended on *Columbia*. He also paid $800,000 the year before for his luxury yacht, a yacht that was costing $30,000 a month to run in the two months of cup-racing time.

As we have seen, with just two days to go, Tommy Lipton, grocer and tea merchant, stood alongside Admiral Dewey, commander of the *Olympia* and national hero of America after his success against the Spanish fleet in the Philippines, in parade. Tommy had already received a salute from the crew of *Olympia*, as ordered by his new friend. Dewey then turned to him and pointed at the gold and jewelled badge that had just been presented to him by a grateful city. 'Sir Thomas,' he said, 'you had better have this, as you seem to get all the cheers.' Even before the match began, Tommy may well have reflected that every penny spent on this challenge in a sport about which he knew next to nothing had been well spent. His day was at hand.

Columbia was waiting. Her waterline length was similar to *Shamrock I*'s, about 90 feet. Unlike *Shamrock I*, however, *Columbia* had been rigorously tested, and not simply on the water to test her speed and handling. Her designer, Nathanael Herreshoff, had experimented with new materials and fittings and, most importantly, how to maximise the sail area. This resulted in massive overhangs, creating greater sail area and, in theory, increased sail power. As Christopher Pastore has pointed out in *Temple to the Wind*, his book about Herreshoff and the 1903 defence, in Herreshoff's designs the ratio of sail area to waterline length had risen from 131:1 for *Vigilant* to 146.5:1 for *Columbia*. However, he observes, 'As the designs became more extreme, steering a ninety footer in a blow or in close quarters could be downright frightening.' Only a few helmsmen were capable of handling such an expanse of sail. Herreshoff knew this, as did J Pierpont Morgan, Edwin D Morgan and Charles Oliver Iselin, the syndicate backing the defence. And even though the crew, who came predominantly from Deer Island, Maine, were not at all happy about it, they had to accept that their skipper and helmsman would be a foreigner, one Charlie

21

Barr. Tommy's Captain Hogarth was going head to head with a fellow Scot.

An air of huge expectation surrounded the match. *Vanity Fair* caught the mood of that first race day in October 1899 when it reported, 'It is a curious thing, yet the fact [is] that this afternoon no one seems to care one little bit about 'The War' . . . The whole Transvaal has dwindled into insignificance on the day of the first race between the *Shamrock* and the *Columbia*.'

In London, at the Embankment, a giant blue billboard had been put up. Upon it were two little yacht hulls, one glowing with a green lamp for *Shamrock I*, the other with a red for *Columbia*, which would be moved along the rails as the races progressed. In this pre-radio age, great crowds gathered to witness the spectacle of these yachting snails. In the event, both they and the thousands who lined the shore and took to the water in New York were to have their enthusiasm sorely tested. The first race, on 3 October, turned into a drifting match and had to be abandoned as it became impossible to complete the course within the time prescribed by the rules. The second attempt went the same way, but at this stage these delays served only to heighten the tension still further. However, when four more matches had to be aborted due either to lack of wind or fog, a real sense of anticlimax pervaded the proceedings.

On 16 October, at 11 a.m. New York time, the starting gun fired. *Shamrock I* had the advantage, crossing the start line first, but just 3 seconds ahead of her rival. The wind had been shifting southerly. For 12 minutes both yachts tacked to starboard, with the wind blowing over the starboard side of each boat. *Shamrock I* switched to a port tack. *Columbia* followed. *Shamrock I* seemed unable to press home her advantage. It was *Columbia* that was pointing higher, lying very close to the wind, and cutting through the water with greater speed. By 1.05 p.m. *Columbia* was 1 mile ahead, with *Shamrock I*'s endeavours to catch her or even reduce her lead proving to be useless. The advantage secured in the windward stretch was pressed home in the leeward leg, *Columbia* running out an easy winner in a 7-knot breeze by a convincing margin of 10 minutes and 8 seconds.

At 11.25 a.m. the following day Tommy was on the bridge of his own steam yacht, *Erin*, standing next to Lord Beresford and Captain Matthews. The second match had started well enough 25 minutes ago. For this first 10-mile leg to windward the east-south-east breeze was brisk. *Shamrock I* had manoeuvred well at the start and for a time the two giants were so close that *Shamrock I*'s mainsail threw a shadow over *Columbia*'s. The boats separated. *Columbia* eased ahead. Then, disaster. In disbelief, Tommy watched as *Shamrock I*'s topmast, the one that carried her biggest club topsail, simply crumpled and collapsed. From that point *Shamrock I* was dead in the water and *Columbia* sailed on to victory. After so many false starts, *Shamrock I* was two down in the blink of an eye and required three straight victories to win the America's Cup. 'The wind was 10 to 14 miles an hour, the kind I desired,' Tommy reflected. 'I had hoped great things from *Shamrock*. Such is the fortune of war. But the contest is not yet over.' After another failure to finish within the time limit on 19 October, a third and decisive contest was completed the following day. Whether beating to windward, running down to leeward, or reaching for the finish line, *Shamrock I* was no match for *Columbia*. She was a mile astern as *Columbia* homed in on the finish. *Columbia*'s design, her technology – her lightweight steel spars, her massive sail area – and, not least, the deft handling by Barr and the experienced crew all contributed to her speed and conquest of *Shamrock I*.

When *Columbia* was within sight of the finish line, her successful defence of the America's Cup virtually assured, Tommy stood up to address his guests over the luncheon table on board *Erin*. As the defeat of *Shamrock I* loomed on the horizon, in this emotionally charged moment, he did not dwell on her shortcomings, or make excuses, or complain about the delays, the weather, or the spectator craft. Instead, Tommy burned with a love of American life and people. His early exposure to American championing of personal merit, hard work and can-do business attitudes had shaped his own philosophy. It had, with no exaggeration, made him what he was.

Although the weight of critical opinion now holds that Tommy's challenges were for commercial gain, on the evidence of what he actually said and did in this period it doesn't seem to have been his sole, or even primary, motivation. In fact, in an unguarded moment before leaving England for this America's Cup challenge, he revealed the depth of his feeling about the Dunraven debacle: when he was asked by an American reporter if he was concerned about the Americans not giving him fair play, he replied curtly, 'It makes my blood boil to hear people even mention such a thing'. He went on, 'What reason is there for suggesting such an abominable idea? The best boat always has won in the past and the best boat is going to win now. The American people always treated former competitors fairly; why should they suddenly behave differently now? . . . I am certain of fair treatment.'

And now, addressing his guests in the moment of defeat several months later, he felt vindicated in his faith. He heaped praise on the American people in general, and complimented the New York Yacht Club on its organisation and, in particular, on the way in which the course was kept clear of any interfering craft. But he went further than that: 'I have surely proved to everyone in England, Scotland and Ireland that if you treat Americans as gentlemen should, they will treat you like gentlemen.'

After the mockery he had received as an outsider and complete novice in British yachting circles – the Royal Yacht Squadron had refused him membership – the long build-up, the vast expense that he had borne alone, the acres of press coverage and the exposure he achieved during Dewey's return, Tommy could have been forgiven for looking and sounding a bit sheepish, but he was neither. First and foremost, he had laid to rest what he saw as the myth that the Americans would in any way conspire to create unfair play. It was as though he was on a personal diplomatic mission to restore both mutual respect and diplomatic relations between Britain and America after the Dunraven episode and in the political contexts of both the Boer and Spanish–American wars.

Secondly, had Tommy been primarily motivated by profit and business success in a rapidly developing market, this was hardly the way to go about it, for all America could see that this British challenger was inferior in every respect. Of course, a counter argument could be that Tommy realised it was his conduct, his name and people saying good things about him that mattered as far as sales were concerned; if he could be seen as the antithesis of Dunraven, he would win no matter what *Shamrock I* did. That may be so. Still, as is clear from many examples in his life, though mindful of positive consequences of his actions, he was not primarily motivated by commercial benefit.

Tommy was certainly impulsive, blessed as he was with boyish enthusiasm throughout his life; he often made snap decisions because he instinctively felt they were right. It would seem unlikely, then, that in the moment of defeat, standing in front of his many guests on board *Erin*, he was thinking about business strategy and financial gain when he said, 'I have had one "go" at the Cup and unless someone else wishes to do so I may have another, but must see my designer before settling anything. For though I can order a yacht, I cannot build one.' The simple truth is probably that he had been thrilled by the whole experience of participating in the America's Cup: the people he had met, the opportunity it had afforded him to entertain and, of course, his pride in almost single-handedly restoring Anglo-American relations. When Sir Henry Burdett stood up to respond to Tommy's speech on behalf of the guests, he said Tommy had lifted something more precious than the cup, namely the goodwill, regard and affection of the American people. And indeed he had.

Before leaving New York after this first, unsuccessful challenge, Tommy was presented with a $5,000, 18-carat gold cup, 14 inches high and set on a green marble base. On it, three mermaids formed handles, from which ran sprigs of shamrock, rose and golden rod, representative of Ireland, England and the United States. Inscribed on the cup were the words '*Amicus Amico*' meaning 'friendly to a friend', and, on another panel, 'To Sir Thomas Lipton From His American Friends, 1899.' That wasn't all. He was made an honorary member of the New York Yacht Club. When he died, Tommy bequeathed this very special trophy back to the club as a gesture of his gratitude. Today, as members of the club look to their left on entering their library, they can see the trophy and be reminded of the great yachtsman and friend of the club, Sir Thomas Lipton.

2

The discovery of America

'As a rule I don't like to look back,' Thomas Lipton maintained. 'I like to look forward. Tomorrow has always been for me a more fascinating day than yesterday or the day before that. The yesterdays have gone; the tomorrows remain.' He railed against people who recounted again and again the achievements of their parents or their illustrious ancestors. For him it was quite simple: 'The only thing that matters is what a man has made of his own life.'

Certainly, as far as his own life was concerned, he believed he was blessed in so many respects in the first fifteen years of his life that the only way he could repay this debt was to continually catapult himself forward and spread good fortune for others in the process. He knew how fortunate he had been and revelled in his reputation for having a positive outlook. Yet, he sometimes allowed vanity to get the better of him, presenting himself as the sole architect of all that he had achieved and forgetting that many different people had helped him along the way. Nevertheless, the origins of his approach to life were sincere and at the core of who he was.

'I am told I am the world's greatest optimist,' he said. 'There's something buoyant and healthy in being an optimist. It is because of my optimism that I have gone through life smiling. That I am always in good humour and good fettle. That I refuse to be gloomy about a lot of trouble that will never happen, whether it is next week or next year.' And at the core of who he was, at the heart of this optimism, was the almost divine figure of his mother.

Frances Johnston was born in 1809 in Clones, County Monaghan, Ireland. She grew up as a simple country girl. Her life was as uncomplicated as the rural landscape around her. It would have continued that way had she not met and fallen in love with a country labourer, an unskilled man by the name of Thomas Lipton.

The Liptons had originally been Scottish farmers and adherents to a strict Calvinist faith, but they had migrated to Ulster and County Fermanagh in the seventeenth century. The Johnstons too had Scottish origins and had settled in Ireland from Dumfriesshire. Over the decades, both families had eked out a basic hand-to-mouth existence from the land, and they intermittently played a part in local, often violent efforts to redress the injustice embodied by the wealthy landlords.

Thomas and Francis married when they were in their twenties, most likely in 1835. They could not have foreseen the famine that was to destroy so many lives in Ireland over the next fifteen years. Between 1845 and 1850 alone, more than 1 million people died of starvation. However, Tommy suggested that the potato famine was not the main reason for his parents' immigration to Scotland in the mid 1840s. In fact, counties Fermanagh and Monaghan – Unionist and drawing in British support as they were – were not as badly affected by the famine as southern Ireland. Tommy implied rather that they left because of an overall agricultural depression. Perhaps the main reason they left was simply because they could. It is possible they knew of other young couples that had made that leap of faith. And they would have found it hard to envisage a better future at home, even though the worst effects of the famine across Ireland were yet to be felt.

Whilst details of Thomas and Frances Lipton's life in the few years up to their departure from Ireland remain very sketchy, it is not diffi-cult to picture Tommy listening to his father later recounting the immense hardships and sacrifices experienced by his mother in this period. A first son was born in 1838. A second son, Christopher, was born in 1840 but died as a baby. A third son was also born in this period but no name was recorded. A daughter, Mary Ann, was born in 1842 but died in 1844. How unutterably hopeless their life must have seemed in Ireland with barely enough to eat, dying children and rumours of even greater hardship around and in front of them.

However, if Frances had, understandably, been emotionally scarred by the harrowing events of her earlier married life, she didn't complain about them to her son and expressed no bitterness. Tommy Senior's main attribute was his devotion to his wife, and in Tommy's own descriptions of his parents there is an imbalance. Here is a man 'clean of heart and clear-eyed' and, in Tommy's own telling phrase about him, 'inclined to be shy and backward'. He may have been, as Tommy also said, more lively and humorous in the company of his own family, but the lasting impression is of a man of little ambition, a man who did not inspire. In contrast, Frances was 'the best, bravest, the noblest mother God ever sent straight from heaven to be one of his angels on earth'. It was not his father but Frances, Tommy said, who 'taught me to hold my head high and to have ideals in life. Honesty, courage and truthfulness were her chief tenets in the philosophy of life. She never tired of impressing these essentials on my young mind.'

Dictating his autobiography to the Scottish journalist Willie Blackwood seventy years later, Tommy was still pondering how she kept a roof over their heads, how she kept going, how she managed to put good meals of soup, porridge and scones on the table on a regular basis. She was 'never idle from morning till night'. Even then, Tommy could honestly say, 'No single day elapses without some fragrant memory of my mother . . . Whatever I am, whatever I possess, whatever I have done – all is due to the little Irish lady from Clones in Ulster. She was my guiding star.'

It was certainly Frances who brought a spiritual dimension into Tommy's life too, insisting on the family's attendance at Hutchesontown Established Church of Scotland in Glasgow's Cleland Street. Tommy confessed that he enjoyed this experience, not least because he perceived at a young age the esteem in which his parents were held. Though he did not adhere to his parents' Protestant faith or practices in his life, he was, nevertheless, always respectful of any denomination or religion that he encountered. He was particular too about the sanctity of Sundays – the one day in the week when business and competition of any sort should be suspended.

Back in the 1840s, before Tommy was even born, only faith and precious little money were sustaining Thomas and Frances when they boarded the ship at Belfast for the short crossing to Glasgow. They travelled with their two surviving children, John and Margaret. Born in 1845, some 60 miles north-east of Clones in County Down, Margaret was not yet three years old. John was nearly ten.

There is no clear record of the family's first days in the crowded metropolis of Glasgow. But if they were going to survive, they had a much better chance here than in their desolate remote cottage in famine-stricken Ireland. And they just happened to be in the right place at the time. The worst economic depression that Britain had experienced, which had claimed the lives of over a million of the poorest people through lack of employment, had ended in 1844.

Added to that, as Britain became more urbanised, a more entrepreneurial middle class developed, and it was from this group that the shopkeepers emerged, their numbers growing with unprecedented speed. Between 1850 and 1870 the number of shopkeepers rose by 54 per cent. Napoleon's barb about Britain being a nation of shopkeepers was prescient indeed.

The Liptons' final stroke of good fortune was in choosing Glasgow itself. Only thirty-five years before its population had been as small as 110,000, but by the 1830s it had risen to 250,000. As the Empire expanded, the city's growth had been powered not merely by shipbuilding in quantity but also by innovations in engineering. It was on the Clyde that the first ships with a screw propeller substituting the paddle were built. It was on the Clyde that iron and then steel were first used in ship production. Within twenty-five years of the Liptons' arrival the Clyde would account for two thirds of all British ship production.

And with Glasgow on the brink of scaling new heights in the late 1840s, in this throbbing boomtown, Thomas, the unskilled labourer from Shannock Green Mills in County Monaghan, could find work. He had an honest face and was clearly not a man more fond of drink than work. He had a succession of jobs, first as a watchman in a cardboard-box warehouse and then later as a timekeeper in a factory where calico was printed.

In this way Thomas and Frances put behind them the daily

uncertainties of Irish rural subsistence, gaining a modest foothold in this vibrant city. And it was into this world they brought their fourth son, Thomas. Here the mystery begins, for rumours of Thomas Johnstone Lipton's birth have been greatly exaggerated. And not least by him.

By his own account he was born on 10 May 1850 in the top four-roomed apartment of a four-storey tenement house in Crown Street in the Gorbals district of Glasgow. He even prefaces this assertion in his autobiography with the sentence, 'Here are the facts.' But the facts cannot be substantiated. The birth of Thomas Lipton is not recorded in the Gorbals register between 1848 and 1850, nor in any other city register. At that time parents were not legally obliged to formally register the births of their offspring. Even so, it is extraordinary that Frances, religious and God-fearing woman that she was, should not have registered her son in a parish register. Even Tommy's assertions that he was born in 1850 and in Crown Street are questionable. The census of 1851 lists him as three years old. The same census does not list the Liptons as living in a tenement in Crown Street or, for that matter, in any other building on Crown Street.

The simplest explanation for Tommy's apparent obfuscation with regard to his birth centres on Frances Lipton, the woman whose maiden name, Johnstone, Tommy later took as a middle name in order to strengthen his association with her. If Tommy genuinely believed he was born on 10 May 1850 in Crown Street it was because she had told him so. For how would he have ever known any different? It was inconceivable for him to doubt her word. Thomas and Frances concealed this hint of their early struggle in Glasgow from Tommy. Perhaps their integrity had been compromised, or they had been dependent on charity. Whatever the reason, Frances chose to say that Crown Street had always been home and that 1850 was the year that life truly began.

As he grew up in the 1850s Tommy hero-worshipped his older brother John, who was sadly rarely in good health. After leaving school, John worked in a chemist's in Virginia Street. It was his dream to become a doctor. To this end he saved money for classes at Glasgow University. But at the age of just nineteen he succumbed to congestion and enlargement of the spleen and liver. His death in August 1857 was a devastating blow for the family. John had been so full of hope and promise. Tommy later wrote of him, 'He was frail in body but full of grit and ambition.'

The family was now reduced to four. Margaret, known at home as Maggie, was a quiet, fragile girl who dutifully followed her mother's instructions, embroidering scarves and handkerchiefs. Maggie was no companion for Tommy in the way that John had been, but even so it is surprising that he barely mentions her in his autobiography. Enrolled in St Andrew's Parish School near Glasgow Green Tommy did not excel as a model pupil and decided in a 'Just William' kind of way that he would learn more from 'life' than lessons. He never lacked confidence or self-esteem, and he was emboldened by his sturdy build and above average height.

One 'life' lesson was taught to him by Willie Ross, a notorious bully and the son of the Crown Street butcher – a boy who collected marbles in the way that the Sheriff of Nottingham collected taxes. Tommy refused to hand over the marbles that he himself had fairly won in a contest. He challenged bigger, stronger, meaner Willie to a fight. It was madness, but Tommy did not back down, and, in a properly conducted bout with rounds and seconds, he fought Willie Ross. To everyone's, especially Willie's, surprise, he lasted six rounds before his seconds conceded defeat. The story as Tommy tells it is one of victory from defeat:

Willie Ross did not trouble him again and he won new respect in the neighbourhood. He learned the valuable lesson that it was possible to win friends and influence people even when, on the face of it, he had lost. By conducting himself with dignity and in a true sporting manner he had come out a winner after all. It was an experience that shaped his approach to the America's Cup.

Tommy's own accounts of what happened to him in his peak teenage years are all at sea, chronologically speaking. He claims to have left school much earlier than he did and to have taken his first proper job at the tender age of ten. A more reliable scenario is that he remained at St Andrew's Parish School, with his parents paying the three pence per week fee, up to the age of fifteen, at which point it seemed more prudent for him to help the stretched family finances rather than go on to further, more expensive schooling at the Hutcheson brothers' new grammar.

Of course by the early 1860s the Liptons were living at 13 Crown Street, and when Tommy was approximately fifteen years of age his parents followed the growing trend by becoming shopkeepers themselves. Their premises was a semi-basement next door to their home, at 11 Crown Street. Thomas Lipton Senior was registered as an egg and butter merchant.

Tommy helped out, sweeping the floor, cleaning around the shop and making helpful suggestions. He advised his father, for example, that his mother should sell the eggs because in her more delicate hands they looked larger and better value. Had Thomas Senior not decided to give up his job at the calico works on MacNeil Street – or, rather, had he not been prompted or encouraged by his wife to establish his own shop – his son would probably never have entered the business that was to make him world-famous; neither would he have developed his

overriding passion for the sea, and every type of vessel which sailed on
it.

It was Tommy's responsibility as a strapping teenager to go to
Lancefield Quay every Monday evening with an empty barrow to
meet the Irish boat that carried the supplies for the Liptons' shop as
well as others. As the boat was never on time and, even once she had
arrived, it took an age to unload her, Tommy had ample opportunity
to wander.

He was totally smitten by the people, the comings and goings, the
different languages, the unusual cargoes, the tobacco and the spices and
the sheer size of the ocean-crossing ships, particularly the American
passenger ships. He spoke to sailors and asked dock labourers about
what they did. Engineers, stevedores, passengers – no one was safe from
his questions about where they had come from and why.

He went to every wharf and dock, marvelling at how the world was
quite literally on his doorstep. 'I bought a cheap map of the world and
found immense delight in tracing the voyages of the various ships –
this one from China, that from Calcutta, the next from Peru.' He had
never learned anything like it in his geography lessons, and he was cap-
tivated, developing 'a passion for ships and shipping and everything
connected with the ocean'. How elated and excited he must have
been, trundling back home over the Jamaica Bridge with his full load
of hams, eggs and butter, dreaming of the sea voyages he could make
when he had enough money.

Tommy's enthusiasm was infectious. He resolved to make his own
model ship and to tell all of his Crown Street friends about it. 'From
the massive lid of an old wooden chest I carved, with infinite labour
and the use of an old "gully" knife, the hull of a boat to which I afterwards added a mast and bowsprit with rigging. The sails I made of

strong paper. When all was shipshape I carried this much treasured craft to a field known as the High Green, not far from Crown Street.'

This was in fact what is now Glasgow Green. And it was here, in giant holes created by earlier brick-making operations which had filled up with water, that Tommy sailed his first, albeit model, yacht. The Crown Street Clan, of which he was the natural leader, responded to his calls for competition. Other sailing craft were constructed out of wooden boxes, and the races began. Immensely proud of his Irish heritage, and no doubt with his mother also in mind, Tommy, or rather the 'Commodore' as he started to be called by his friends, named his yacht *Shamrock*.

Although *Shamrock* was often a winner, these boyish escapades didn't really satisfy Tommy's appetite for the sea. He had to experience the thrill of being on the water himself. To that end he spent any extra few pence he ever had on hiring a small cut-boat, on learning the rhythm of oars and even on sailing a lugsail boat on the Clyde. But he rarely had very much money and these indulgences were not nearly as frequent as he would have liked.

Outside of his parents' shop Tommy's first successful foray into the world of work was with Glassford Street stationers A & W Kennedy. The salary, however, amounted to little more than pennies and the work was as dull as the docks were exciting. He left, having earned half a crown for six days' work. Ever the opportunist, he spied an opening at Messrs Tillie & Henderson, a large and reputable firm of shirtmakers. They were housed literally round the corner from Glassford Street, in Miller Street. Yet here too Tommy was uninspired. This time, however, he had to grit his teeth and get on with his given task because the pay was twice as good as at Kennedys'. For a fifteen-year-old boy dreaming of long sea journeys and stepping on America's shores, cutting out shirt patterns and making them into sample books for salesmen was a truly mind-numbing activity.

The chores for his parents' shop, followed by the tedium of Kennedys' and the repetition of shirt patterns at Tillie & Henderson did not make for the most gratifying or stimulating occupations. Unsurprisingly, there is no sense at all from Tommy that during this period he was particularly attracted by the notion of working in a retail environment. Apart from his comment about his mother selling eggs, nothing else he says suggests that he was interested in shops or serving customers.

In a final fling with formal education Tommy also attended the Gorbals Youth School after he had completed each day's work at Tillie & Henderson. In an uncharacteristic piece of character assassination he later referred to Thomas Neil, who ran the school, as 'a crusty, ill-tempered old crank who wore big-rimmed blue spectacles and was known to everyone in the district as "Auld Specky"'. Tommy was not a reader of books and he would have probably missed out, for example, on the remarkable success of *Tom Brown's Schooldays* published in 1857, or even Charles Dickens' *Great Expectations*, published in 1861. Auld Specky, though, conjures up an image of a master of Rugby School or even one of Dickens' great characters, David Copperfield's cane-wielding headmaster, Mr Treacle.

Then an opportunity to escape Auld Specky and shirt patterns presented itself: Tommy heard that the Burns Line was looking for a cabin boy to serve on its passenger ships between Glasgow and Belfast, for the princely sum of 8 shillings a week. He talked his way into the position, leaving lessons and shirts to embark on a new career at sea. Though he was still a general dogsbody, the pay was better at sea and he had the opportunity to learn from people of different backgrounds.

The tips were good too, and he had a chance to put some money aside at last.

It was too good to continue for long. On a chance inspection in the early spring of 1866, a shore steward discovered a cabin lamp that had been allowed to smoke, blackening a ceiling. It was an unforgivable offence, for a cabin boy at least, and Tommy was given his marching orders. Tommy just shrugged his shoulders and left. The job had served its purpose. He now knew all about the great ships that set sail from the Clyde, such as the formidable *United States*, with her 1,200-ton displacement, single funnel, three masts and full sail. Launched in 1860, she ran a fortnightly service to New York. The Anchor Line's *Devonia* was also a regular on the United States run. Now Tommy had amassed enough spare money and built enough resolve to be able to announce his intention to his parents.

What a shock it must have been for Thomas and Frances to hear their only surviving son and source of assured income declare categorically that his mind was made up to go to New York. Certainly, home would be a lot quieter at the end of the day, with no more tales of the sailors he had encountered at Lancefield Quay and anecdotes about overheard conversations whilst crossing the Irish Sea. Thomas knew their son and refusing him wasn't really an option. Though he would return and his parents and Maggie would be there waiting for him, Tommy had put the lid on the box of his childhood forever. But, of course, he could carry it around with him, opening it now and again, drawing strength from it and allowing it to influence his whole approach to life.

His daydreams had often carried him off to New York, but now that the crowded reality loomed large in front of the bow of the ship

Tommy wasted no time in either savouring the moment or succumbing to any fears about the enormity of his decision. He was an impetuous teenager and one who knew that the 30 shillings in his pocket would not last long.

Not surprisingly, Tommy had befriended many of his fellow travellers during the two-week Atlantic crossing, many of them Irish families. They were as unsure as he was of what to expect on arrival in New York, and even before their ship, the *Caledonia*, had tied up at Castle Gardens on Manhattan Island, Tommy had spotted an opportunity to be their self-appointed agent. He had noticed on the quayside a band of hoteliers and boarding-house keepers promoting their establishments to other recently arrived immigrants.

Tommy quickly formulated his plan and, like a greyhound out of the traps, bolted for the gangway, making sure he was one of the first to disembark. Mike McCauligan, whose boarding house was at 27 Washington Street, became his first target. In no time at all he had persuaded Mr McCauligan to give him free board for a week if he could secure a dozen paying guests. This was of course not difficult for an enterprising fellow like Tommy. He had thus overcome his first major obstacle in the New World – finding a place to stay without depleting his sparse funds.

The next task was to find a job but, strangely, success here proved elusive. Through an agency, he eventually secured an offer of work, not in New York but as a labourer on a tobacco plantation in Virginia. Only a year had passed since Virginia's most famous and admired son, General Robert E Lee, had surrendered the Confederate cause to Ulysses S Grant at Appomattox. It was only a year, too, since the bullet of John Wilkes Booth had passed through the head of Abraham Lincoln at Ford's Theater in Washington, ending his life and, arguably, hopes of a more positive reconstruction after the Civil War of 1861 to 1865.

Virginia had been the focus of much military action in this bloody conflict over slavery and secession. The Union's headlong rush to Virginia's capital, Richmond, in 1861, ended in humiliating defeat at Bull Run. General McClellan's endeavour to capture Richmond the following year resulted in failure since the tactical brilliance of Lee forced him to withdraw in seven days. Lee inflicted a second defeat on the Union at Bull Run in August 1862, but his own defeat at Gettysburg in the summer of 1863 was to prove a turning point in the war.

Of these recent events, of the physical scars on the landscape, of the broken-bodied boys of his own age in evidence on every street corner, Tommy says nothing in his memoirs. It is truly remarkable that he should find himself in the killing fields of Virginia, where the sound of cannon fire had ceased only months before, and not make any reference to it. We cannot know whether he was deeply moved by what he witnessed in Virginia, whether his experiences planted seeds in his subconscious that grew in time into a deep compassion for people of any colour or creed caught in the crossfire of politics, poverty and war. Perhaps memories of his time in Virginia were too painful to recall, or perhaps, equally, he was too wrapped up in his own quest to avoid poverty and make his way to register much else. Either way, his trip to Virginia would have been a new experience for him: the people he met were not the jolly well-to-do Americans he had met on the Broomielaw in Glasgow or the fast-talking salesmen of New York, but the victims of suffering and hardship on a scale he had not encountered before.

Picking tobacco leaves, all day, every day, under the hot Virginian sun was physical, backbreaking work. If the state was to recover from the devastation of war, its tobacco, coal-mining and textile industries needed to be revitalised. From plantation-owner Sam Clay's perspective, Tommy was an ideal labourer: hard-working, trustworthy and with no baggage from the war. And Tommy was up for it, at least for a short while. It didn't take him long to realise that there was no variety in the work and little prospect of any advancement. In short, it was a dead-end job and he resolved to move on in a matter of weeks.

Tommy was drawn once more to New York where, in theory at least, his prospects were brighter, but again he was re-directed south by a New York agency, this time to Chisholm Island, further south, on the South Carolina coast. The job consisted of more hard labour, this time on a rice plantation, and here, he spent the winter of 1867–68. Cheerful, articulate and numerate, he stood out, and he soon escaped from the drudgery of work in the fields. However, his escape was due less to his working abilities, and more to his becoming the confidant of the Spaniard with whom he lodged. The Spaniard, who remains nameless, had married an Irish girl, who also lived with them in a bizarre *ménage à trois*. But the two-timing Spaniard was continuing a correspondence with a previous girlfriend, a Charleston belle. In one of the worst decisions of his life, Tommy agreed to help the Spaniard with the correspondence to his mistress in Charleston. When the Irish wife discovered the letters, the Spaniard thought Tommy had betrayed him and went after him with a knife.

Needless to say, this tale of lust and revenge was one of Tommy's most treasured anecdotes, to be used for entertainment in the right company. It receives due embellishment in his autobiography: 'The hot-blooded Spaniard convinced that I had betrayed him, turned on me and before I realised what was happening he had drawn a knife from his belt and slashed me with it. Only my agility and fleetness of foot prevented me from being murdered. Dodging the infuriated man, I rushed to the door and out of the cabin. He pursued me all the way to the overseer's house. Fortunately, Mr Matthews, the overseer, was on the spot and he not only gave me instant shelter, but held off the enraged Spaniard with a loaded revolver.' The hot-blooded Spaniard had cooled down by the following morning and apologised. Magnanimously, Tommy forgave him, and Mr Matthews, impressed with Tommy's conduct, rewarded him with a new desk-bound administrative role that was principally book-keeping. Overnight, he had, thanks to the slashing Spaniard, graduated from labourer to accountant.

This is the last detailed adventure in Tommy's discovery of the war-torn states of America. Of his life at the rice plantation the *Charleston News* later reported, 'The young foreigner worked for a year, but after a disagreement with the plantation foreman he took a "bateau" and left.' By his own vague account Tommy then stopped here and there doing odd jobs in different, unspecified states and even ending up as a tram driver in New Orleans. In all likelihood he was restless, not earning steady money and increasingly feeling like a fish out of water. Surely he would be able to make a better go of things in New York – after all, it felt closer to home and it was more like the city life he knew, albeit on a larger scale.

Back in New York, Tommy was third time lucky, finding work in the grocery section of a store. And it wasn't just any corner store in the myriad of New York side streets: his employer was in fact an Ulster man, Alexander Turney Stewart, whose fashionable department store in Manhattan was well regarded. While Tommy had no real thoughts of emulating his parents at this point, the job being more important as a means to a steady wage than as a career path, the contrast between this slick grocery operation and his parents' tiny shop was too great to ignore. Stewart's was bigger for a start. Even this grocery section, just part of the larger department store, was much larger than his parents' shop, which could not hold more than six people at any one time. Stewart's was bright too, and though the hams, cheeses and breads were not so different from those he had seen at home, they were displayed more imaginatively, and in such quantity, items piled high on spotlessly clean counters.

The biggest difference, however, was in customer sevice – not that his parents were unfriendly or that the salesmen of Kennedys' and Tillie & Henderson had been abrupt or rude. They just weren't that keen on selling, and the onus was always on the customer to decide and demand. Here, though, greater emphasis was placed on the way sales staff presented themselves. It mattered that they knew everything about what was on sale and what the special offers were. They engaged customers who strayed on to their shop floor with friendly conversation, and they encouraged them to buy.

Tommy wanted to absorb all that he could from the school of Stewart's and earn as much as possible, not simply to book his return to Scotland – for which he needed $500 – but also to give him enough capital to start up on his own. A changed man, his dreams of crossing oceans and travelling to exotic places had been supplanted by a new vision of the future. By this time, late into 1869, he was missing his mother, especially. He had formed no known romantic liaisons whilst in America, and he simply wanted to be reunited with her. His goal in going back was not to re-live the past, but to show the one person he cared about most how he was going to create the future. And if he had drawn strength and energy from idealised memories of childhood on his American odyssey, he was now charged up with inspiration and ideas for his return to Scotland.

The American approach to life, their war and peace, their hardship and prosperity, had taught him lessons in self-sufficiency. He had been possessed of a vitality and self-confidence before, but his exposure to American life in all its colours and challenges gave him a new impetus that went far beyond the basic prerequisites for survival and into the realms of go-getting.

Tommy made his triumphant return to Glasgow, bearing the not inconspicuous gifts of flour and a rocking chair. From the docks, he instructed the driver of his cab to take the longer route round to Crown Street and not to rush. It was abundantly clear that he was keen to let Glasgow know he had returned. To put it bluntly, he was full of himself.

His parents' intial euphoria at his return was quickly tempered by Tommy's revelation of his plans to open his own shop. They did not share his desire to make people sit up and take notice of the Lipton name. They didn't want to draw attention to themselves, to advertise or stoop to other methods of promotion. It was vulgar, vain and against their principles.

In the April 1871 census Tommy was still registered as living with his parents in Crown Street. A claim has also been made by James Mackay in his 1998 biography of Lipton that in 1871 he had formed a romantic attachment with a Catholic girl, nineteen-year-old Margaret McAuslan, and that they were married in May 1871 in St Francis' Catholic Church in the Gorbals by Father Brendan Butti with witnesses – but not Tommy's parents – in the same week that Tommy opened his first shop.

Moreover, the marriage is thought to have been precipitated by

Margaret's pregnancy; on Christmas Day 1871, a son, Tom, is said to have been born. Tom lived briefly and died, Mackay claims, of a bilious fever on 6 November 1872. A second son, William, was then born on 15 September 1873, and this seemingly unhappy event necessitated the dispatch of Margaret and baby William to Canada, leaving no further trace of their whereabouts.

These are extraordinary claims, particularly as in later life Tommy denied all press rumour-mongering that he had ever been married. He made his denials in his usual good-humoured and jocular fashion, but they were categorical denials nonetheless: 'No, sir, I've never married because I cannot reconcile myself to the thought of just one wife.' And, around the same time, speaking of American women in particular, 'I like them all. I couldn't seem to choose among them so I didn't choose at all.'

In this and other interviews given to the American press at this time he spoke of his 'one love' and invariably reached for the picture of his mother that was close to hand. He was so well practised in this media game that it was never a problem disarming even the most inquisitive journalist with mom-and-apple-pie tales. 'It wasn't only the pancakes she used to fry and the pies she used to bake, it was the sweetness and wisdom of her. Never a time did I go to her in trouble that she didn't help me. Course she's gone now, but I had got somewhere near the top, thank heaven, and I repaid her a little. I used to tell her she could have a dozen fine carriages if she wanted them, but she never wanted much, more's the pity.'

More's the pity too that Frances left no trace of any letters Tommy had sent to her from America in the 1860s. Had he told her of any romantic liaisons in Virginia, South Carolina or even New York? Sadly, about the years from his discovery of America to the opening of his first shop in 1871, years that shaped the direction of his life, there is very little clarity and few incontrovertible facts. We only have his woolly and selective accounts narrated to Willie Blackwood and other journalists years later.

Given Tommy's own evasiveness and other inaccuracies in accounts of his life, it is understandable that this secret marital issue should give rise to speculation about his whole character. However, it is possible to debunk some of the speculation. The parish register of St Francis's for May 1871 is abundantly clear: Friar Butti did marry Thomas Lipton and Margaret McAuslan on 12 May 1871 with witnesses, but not *the* Thomas Lipton. The groom was a coalminer and son of William and Mary Lipton. He died in 1902 at the age of 50 and his death certificate clearly states that he was 'married to Margaret McAuslan'.

It is perhaps too easy to judge Tommy harshly for his secrecy about his private life, a secrecy that begins in this period. It is as though he made a conscious decision on this first American adventure, in his first genuine taste of freedom, to keep his own counsel, and it is perfectly possible that he revelled in his anonymity in America and formed attachments, however brief. He was, after all, a red-blooded teenager free from the constraints of home. And whatever he may have done on his return, he certainly didn't marry Margaret McAuslan; his mother was, and remained, the focal point of his life.

For now, back in Glasgow and possessed of a vision for the future that he had formed in America, it was time to deliver – to demonstrate to his old world that his discovery of the New World had changed him forever.

3

Columbia, the second challenge, 1901

Larry Ellison, the Chicago-born co-founder of software giant Oracle and head of the Oracle BMW Racing 2003 America's Cup syndicate, observes, 'The start is critical in match racing. Winning the start does not necessarily mean that they started in front of us. It means that they got the side of the racecourse that they wanted. Five minutes before the race begins, both boats decide which side of the racecourse has the better wind conditions: more wind and/or a favourable wind shift up the course. If both boats pick the same side of the course, they fight for it by executing a complex set of manoeuvres with each boat trying to gain a right-of-way advantage against the other. This five minute manoeuvring period before the start is called the pre-start. It's the most exciting part of match racing.'

Ellison is referring to his team's duel with the Swiss yacht, *Alinghi*, in the first semi-final of the Louis Vuitton Cup, the all-important series of match races in the modern America's Cup that determines which team will be the challenger to the defender. Winning the start ten out of twelve times, *Alinghi* defeated Ellison's Oracle BMW Racing team and went on to become the first ever European winner of the America's Cup. It was of little consolation to Larry Ellison to receive a sympathetic email from America's Cup legend and fellow American Dennis Conner. His own Team Dennis Conner, representing the New York Yacht Club, had been eliminated at the quarter-final stage. Conner was, though, already guaranteed a prominent place in America's Cup history: he had sailed *Freedom* to victory over Alan Bond's *Australia*, but then lost the Auld Mug three years later sailing *Liberty* against Allan Bond's revolutionary winged-keel, Ben Lexcen-designed *Australia II*. Conner was to reclaim the America's Cup for the United States by sailing *Stars and Stripes* to victory off the western Australian coast in 1987.

Dennis Conner's own America's Cup career had begun in some style in 1974 when he became starting helmsman and tactician on the successful *Courageous*, headed by the flamboyant and linguistically colourful media mogul Ted Turner. *Courageous* won again in 1977, skippered that year by Ted Hood. In Conner's own successes in the years that followed, his alleged disruptive bullying tactics of crowding out an opponent in the pre-start became a trademark of his sailing and a key feature in many of his victories. Less well known is the fact that Conner modelled himself on a man who had defended the America's Cup more than seventy years before him. This man had played no small part in thwarting Tommy Lipton in 1899. Even worse, from Lipton's perspective, was that this captain had been born in Scotland. He had even gained his first cup experience as mate on board the unsuccessful 1887 challenger of the Royal Clyde Yacht Club, *Thistle*. On that occasion his older half brother John was skipper. But when *Thistle* was sold several years later to Kaiser Wilhelm II, he left Scotland for America, where he worked as a professional captain. His name was Charlie Barr.

Barr had endured his share of defeats: when he skippered *Vigilant* as one of the yachts competing to defend the America's Cup he was soundly beaten by Hank Haff on *Defender*. Hardened by such experiences, Charlie applied a new rigour and discipline to his already unsentimental leadership. Tough by nature and tough by example, he commanded his crews of mixed abilities and nationalities with an authority that belied his own diminutive frame. Just as Charlie made sure he got every last ounce of effort from his crew, he also scrutinised the race rule book for every possible advantage, and the pre-start tactics he deployed as a result had the Cup Committee constantly reaching for their own copies. With complete confidence in his tamed crew, an instant recollection of the most effective sail combinations in tight manoeuvres, a single-minded decisiveness and an arrogant confidence in the limits of engagement, Barr would harry his opponent, driving his own yacht on to her windward quarter, crowding her out, forcing her away from the start line. For Barr the pre-start wasn't simply a question of finding the most favourable position and side from which to begin the race, it was also a matter of putting his opponent at the greatest disadvantage.

Charlie Barr's great strength was that he carefully considered every source of competitive advantage for the race, from beginning to end. His was a hard-edged professionalism that put winning above every other consideration. He was paid handsomely for his work – as much as $3,500 for a single America's Cup summer – but he could be as brusque with his paymasters as the men under his command, and from his point of view he was there to get a job done.

49

Major Heckstall Smith, the celebrated British yachtsman, writer and friend of Tommy Lipton, sailed with Barr often and recounts how he never let his concentration slip, even when comfortably ahead. Nothing annoyed Charlie more than slacking or inattention. When Heckstall Smith told him once during a race that they couldn't possibly lose it, Barr replied in good humour, 'I'm never content. We may be too far ahead and run into a calm and other yachts will sail around us. For goodness sake, sir, take your glasses and look ahead on the water for calm patches.'

It is no wonder, then, that Dennis Conner and other America's Cup yachtsmen have been inspired by Charlie Barr down the years. In the late 1950s, Bus Mosbacher – skipper of the so-called America's Cup superboat *Intrepid* and later chief of protocol in President Nixon's administration – mastered, and some say invented, a manoeuvre of chasing his adversary from the starting line, with the appearance of a dog chasing its tail. But this 'tail chasing' was, as Conner has pointed out, really a technique originated and perfected by Barr. Charlie employed it to the greatest effect in the trial races for the 1899 America's Cup, against Herreshoff's latest creation, *Constitution*, captained by Uriah Rhodes, a top-rate seaman who had been a mate and skipper on the *Defender* in the previous trials against *Columbia* in 1898.

The America's Cup had become an obsession for Tommy Lipton: 'I am eating, drinking, sleeping Cup' he was happy to tell the American press. He had, he declared, given carte blanche to his appointed designer of the new challenger, *Shamrock II*: 'What I want is the best possible boat, the best boat that British materials and brains can turn out.' Even a master of timing and publicity like him had been surprised by the warmth and goodwill his first challenge had aroused, but what had surprised him more was how deeply he had felt the defeat of *Shamrock I*. He had been convinced that she was a better boat than *Columbia* but, as he remarked on the outcome of the decisive match, '*Columbia* showed herself to be the better ship in a spanking whole-sail breeze', and 'almost before the "gun" in that final race I had resolved to have another "cut" for the Cup'. There is no doubt that he badly wanted to win, and vanity also got the better of him: he wanted more of the adulation. If he could be given a gold cup, honorary membership of the New York Yacht Club, the freedom of Chicago, the status of honorary chief of the New York Police and 'honorary membership of the New York Athletic Club, the most wonderful organisation of its kind in the world', the first time around, who knew what might happen in future challenges. If he could entertain one Guglielmo Marconi and play a part in his first ship-to-shore wireless experiments simply by being in the right place at the right time and by virtue of being the challenger for the America's Cup, it is not surprising that he was not long in confirming his second challenge. Of Marconi he later reflected in his autobiography, 'I always think, in view of what radio has come to mean in our lives today, that this was one of the most interesting features of my first yacht racing in American waters.'

And now, in the early winter of 1900, he was leaving business correspondence to one side as much as he possibly could to focus on his next challenge, delivered to and accepted by the New York Yacht Club in the previous autumn. Just how animated or obsessed Tommy was becoming about the cup at this time is evidenced by strident views he expressed in the media. Although he was happy to proclaim Americans as the finest yachtsmen alive, he was also aware of a new extravagant presence on the America's Cup scene, Thomas Lawson from Boston, who was determined to build his own cup defender. Lawson, like

Lipton himself, was not a member of the New York Yacht Club. But there the similarity ended. Lawson was a financial speculator, the 'copper king' who made spectacular gains in copper shares, a man of extreme behaviour who always gambled on stupendous odds at the risk of losing everything. The yacht he commissioned, named *Independence* and designed by Boudoin Crowninshield, a Harvard-educated and adventurous yacht designer, would mirror his business approach of operating in extremes, always gambling on great financial success at the risk of losing everything. *Independence* was constructed of nickel steel and aluminum alloy as well as the Tobin bronze used in plating her hull. Launched on 17 May 1901, she measured 140 feet overall with a waterline length of 90 feet. Her massive sails, fully unfurled, covered an area of 14,611 square feet, compared with 13,135 for *Columbia* and 13,485 for *Shamrock II*. By contrast, a hundred years later, America's Cup yachts have a mainsail area of approximately 2,365 square feet and a spinnaker fully spread of 5,380 square feet.

From his office in the Worthington Building in State Street Lawson conducted his ultimately fruitless campaign for the New York Yacht Club to allow his yacht, *Independence*, to compete in the cup-defence trials without actually representing the club. The point was that it was the America's Cup and not, as Lawson wished to interpet it, America's cup – that is, open to all Americans to defend.

It was no coincidence that in the same month – December 1900 – of heightened American press speculation about the construction at the cost of several hundred thousand dollars of Thomas Lawson's *Independence* and the New York Yacht Club-approved *Constitution*, designed by Herreshoff, Tommy should author an article in the *Boston Post* on the need for simplicity in yacht racing. Always eager to position himself as the people's champion on both sides of the Atlantic, he rails against the cost of both cup challengers and cup defenders, not wishing to point the finger at the Americans or single out any individual for criticism. He calls the America's Cup-competing yachts 'mere racing machines, constructed at enormous cost for a single effort, and after that, useless'. He doesn't stop there.

'We discard wood for hulls and make use of fancy metals that cost almost as much as gold and which soon lose their power to resist the action of the sea. And this merely to gain a little lightness. We have suits of sails that cost as much as the total outlay for cup challengers and defenders of a few years ago, and the cost of present-day contestants must be many times those of a few years ago.' Tommy admits that this may seem strange coming from him but argues that the Americans 'are ready to expend ten dollars to every one of mine in order that they shall not lose the Cup. I believe they will spare no pains, no expense of construction in the turning out of a racing yacht that will defend their valued prize.' He has, therefore, no choice but 'to make use of the same tactics and endeavour if brains and money can avail to improve upon them'. He does not venture any solution to this problem as he sees it, other than to call for a return to sailing basics and a mutually agreed abandonment of 'certain extraordinary extravagances'.

This styling of himself as the underdog, as the man to remind all that this was meant to be a simple yachting contest between friendly nations and as the millionaire who still knew the price of half a dozen eggs was as tactical as any of Charlie Barr's pre-start manoeuvres. He delighted in putting clear blue water between himself and the faceless charisma-free great American industrialists that financed the defence of the cup.

Contempt might be too strong a word, but it is not difficult to imagine the private disregard of Messrs JP and ED Morgan, backing the defence once more, for such a romanticised technology-reduced vision of America's Cup racing. From their perspective, the whole point was to showcase a nation's skills – and, understandably, American supremacy – and use every available design enhancement to produce the biggest, best and fastest yachts.

Yet Tommy was adamant. Not for the first time in his life he had thrown his whole self into something he fully believed in. In this case he saw the America's Cup as the pinnacle of a sport that should be of and for the people. As such it should set an example of skill, enduring construction, sportsmanlike competition and reasonable cost. In other words, the extremes of the new breed of America's Cup yachts and other competing international yachts were having a detrimental impact on the take-up and enthusiasm for the sport at every level. As he put it, 'The great increase in the cost of Cup racing cannot fail to be felt eventually by everyone in any way connected with yachting . . . It will soon come about that the man with an ordinary boat cannot hope to compete against the racing machines constructed for the excessively rich.' Tommy genuinely did not want yachting to be the preserve of royalty or the super rich, though he was now one of their number. Given a choice, he would side with the working class. He was one of them after all and they were, so to speak, his bread and butter. However, he would not use his wealth or international status to be judgemental in any class battle.

That said, he also made it his personal goal to improve the very strained Anglo-American relations of recent years. In almost every public utterance he went out of his way to applaud the gentleman-liness and the sailing prowess of the Americans. Tommy even expressed 'the hope that the year 2000 will witness the same friendly, honorable and exciting races for the America's Cup as those which mark the beginning of this century'. He would not have rejoiced in the bitter disputes and name-calling that have erupted in the last quarter century, prompting one writer, Doug Riggs, to entitle his 1980s book *Keelhauled: Unsportsmanlike Conduct and the America's Cup*. There have indeed been some shocking examples of bad sportsmanship, fanning the flames of the cup's notoriety. They have, it could be said, given the event an edge, one that it wouldn't have if everyone behaved like Lipton. As his fame spread in America, more than a few journalists bemoaned the fact that it was impossible to dislike him. The contrast to the Dunraven experience could not have been greater. Nobody in America wanted to give Lipton a bloody nose or to put the British in their place by humiliating him: he was too nice.

Of course, whatever his idealised view of yachting as a sport for and of the people, Tommy knew his ability to influence its future direction would increase a hundredfold were he to win the America's Cup for the Royal Ulster Yacht Club, for Britain and for himself. In October 1900 he told the *New York Herald*, 'I would give every penny I have and begin again at the bottom of the ladder to lift the America's Cup.'

Tommy placed his faith in three men in particular. The first of these, his designer George Watson, had contributed to the design of earlier failed challengers, namely *Thistle* and two of the Earl of Dunraven's *Valkyries*. Even so, he had, since setting up in business in 1872 as a naval architect, enjoyed considerable success in designing race winners in British waters. Most notable among these was the Prince of Wales's *Britannia*. In building his reputation he had enjoyed the early patronage of James Coats, the celebrated and wealthy threadmill owner of Paisley. Watson combined a naval architect's precision with scientific experimentation in his designs. He fervently believed in the merits of testing. Coming out of retirement at Lipton's request, he dusted off his wax modelling technique and turned again to his partnership with the physicist William Froude. Watson took a dim view of the syndicate responses of the Americans, which he said had 'neither soul to be damned nor body to be kicked. Surely there is enough wealth to spare in the United States for one gentleman to undertake the duty and pleasure of defending the Cup.' He was, nevertheless, more than gracious in his praise of the Herreshoffs, believing them capable of building a yacht 10 minutes faster than the 1899 defender, *Columbia*. But could he beat them? 'God knows. I don't,' he remarked.

Lipton's second talisman was Captain Edward Sycamore, a forty-year-old native of Brightlingsea on the English Essex coast. He was pigeonholed early by the American press, who invariably described him as 'a bluff, hearty, typical English seaman', but Sycamore was no lightweight. He had sailed on both *Valkyrie II* and *Valkyrie III* in the 1890s. In the 1900 yachting season he had taken command of *Mineola*, the flying racing yacht of top New York businessman and New York Yacht Club member August Belmont. In the sea-focused community of Brightlingsea, where captains occupied the better houses at the top of the town and had special drinking areas reserved for them in the local pubs, Sycamore was revered. In the wider local area, too, he was greatly respected and was even made deputy to the Mayor of Sandwich.

The third man was Willie Jameson, a widely acknowledged, gifted Irish yachtsman who had taken the helm of *Britannia* when *Vigilant* had raced her in British waters. Jameson's role would be as manager of *Shamrock II* and adviser to both Lipton and Watson. Jameson was noted for his cunning, his intuition in reading currents and tides, his knowledge of the sky and, perhaps above all, his fearlessness. In short, he was a formidable competitor and one rated by the Americans. His opposite number on *Columbia*, Charles Oliver Iselin, had noted that 'he is as good as five minutes to any boat'.

Watson, Sycamore and Jameson. Were they a strong enough combination to lead a winning challenge for Tommy? Would *Shamrock II* succeed where *Shamrock I* had failed? However much Tommy and his top team of advisers might have wanted to face a defender funded by one individual or participate in a match that was not powered by the most expensive materials, they had to accept the status quo and compete. Tommy certainly believed he had got it all wrong with their first challenge. His team had, he noted, been hindered by William Fife's illness: Fife's rheumatic fever in New York had even made it impossible for him to oversee *Shamrock I*'s final measurement. He had been so ill that he had not been told the outcome of the races until two days after the challenge had failed. But Tommy professed his confidence in winning this second time and it was time to show his hand.

Under a soft blue spring sky, on an April Saturday of summer temperatures, *Shamrock II* was launched. Thousands had gathered at the Dumbarton shipyard of William Denny and Brothers, both on shore and on a flotilla of small craft, to witness the event.

On his arrival at 11 a.m. on 20 April, Tommy immediately took charge of the assembled pressmen, escorting them to the shed enclosing the new challenger. Only her keel and bulb were concealed. The Marchioness of Dufferin, in harmony with Sir Thomas's other principal guests, including her husband – the commodore of the Royal Ulster Yacht Club and former governor general of Canada, who was to become the British ambassador to France – was sporting a spray of shamrock. High on a platform draped in red and yellow, she christened *Shamrock II* with a bottle of wine amid cheers and hooting sirens. Atop

Shamrock II as she slid into the River Clyde, Tommy's own racing flag, with St Patrick's flower at its centre, fluttered in the breeze. Fore and aft flew the lion of Scotland and the burgee of the Royal Ulster Yacht Club, the red hand of Ulster surmounted by a crown on a white background.

In the midst of the jubilations and the congratulatory optimism, a Herreshoff was watching. Not Captain Nat, but his son Francis Herreshoff, who declared that *Shamrock II* was a creditable boat but was, in analysis, only a second *Meteor* – Kaiser Wilhelm's racing yacht. 'Summing up all her points, good and bad, I should say she is too small for what she measures. American boats of the same measurement have invariably been more powerful than their British-built challengers and *Shamrock II* perpetuates this defect.'

This was, however, a harsh judgement in comparison with other comments. American yachting expert John R Spears declared that she was the smartest challenger ever to cross the Atlantic. Tommy was especially pleased to hear this as Spears was respected in yachting circles and had heavily criticised *Shamrock I*.

In truth, she was a big improvement, designed more to skim the water than to plough through it; the harsh angles were notably absent and her lines curved smoothly up from her hull. Above her pine-covered aluminium deck, her main mast was a steel tube into which the topmast, also of yellow pine, could be telescoped. If she had been brought up in full sail alongside Tower Bridge in London, her mast would have risen nearly 30 feet over the top platform, which stands at 142 feet.

In her trials *Shamrock II* had mixed fortunes. That she could sail through variable light breezes, gathering speed and skimming over the water's surface, was amply demonstrated on the Solent. That she was

accident-prone was also proven. The same day the *Yachting World* published an article praising her speed, 9 May 1901, her sail and rigging
came off the main mast and, along with a turning block, clattered on
to the deck when Tommy was on board. More drama was to follow
only weeks later when Tommy's most important friend was on
Shamrock II.

In *Leaves from the Lipton Logs* Tommy devotes a number of pages to
his friend King Edward VII. The king, 'one of my most sincere well-
wishers' in the America's Cup, had, says Tommy, previously allowed his
own yacht, *Britannia*, to test *Shamrock I* in trials when no other yacht
was available. He refers to him in glowing terms as a man with a keen
sense of humour. The king preferred informality, in yachting excur-
sions at least, and it was his custom 'to take a kindly view of any . . .
incident or mishap no matter how serious the personal inconvenience
caused to himself'.

This was just as well, for the king was on board *Shamrock II* when
she dismasted during her trials with *Shamrock I* and *Sybarita*. The king
viewed the calamity from the companionway and was unhurt. If anything, he seemed to relish the unscheduled commotion. He remained
for dinner on the *Erin* that evening and entertained the company with
his version of events – all in good humour at Tommy's expense of course.

None of these problems dented Tommy's confidence. He was satisfied with his second *Shamrock*, his team of Watson, Sycamore, Jameson
and his crew of thirty-eight – none of whom were Scottish, but four-
teen of whom were seasoned Brightlingsea men like Edward
Sycamore. On departure from Liverpool on 13 August he declared that
Shamrock II was going to win. He was, though, as surprised as anybody
that his *Shamrock* would face Charlie Barr, once more at the helm of
Columbia: 'I hope we are going to meet their very best boat for, win or

lose, I should like to feel that I am racing against the best America can produce.'

The trials of the challenger were in fact tame compared with the battle that took place to decide the defender of the America's Cup. The unholy row between Thomas Lawson and the New York Yacht Club, articulated in superficially polite correspondence and less polite advertising campaigns, did not culminate in a showdown on the water. Forbidden by the New York Yacht Club from participating in approved trial races, *Independence* had to compete in a separate unofficial match with other contenders. But here she was humiliated. Steering problems, a lack of balance and her sheer size rendered her unpredictable and at times uncontrollable in racing conditions. In disgust, Lawson had her scrapped in September, even before the official defence actually began.

To the business yachting cognoscenti, this was not entirely surprising. What was, however, was Nat Herreshoff's failure to design a yacht that could better *Columbia*. A six-strong syndicate that included two Vanderbilts and was headed by Vice Commodore August Belmont – who was, of course, well known to Edward Sycamore – funded the creation of Herreshoff's *Constitution*. That she would become the new defender was virtually taken for granted. However, although the eighteen trial races resulted in honours even, Barr's pre-start tactics, along with his marshalling of his crew and, in turn, their responsiveness to him from start to finish, made the decision for the Cup Committee. For the first time in America's Cup history the same yacht would defend the America's Cup a second time.

The *Columbia* was jointly owned by three men: JP Morgan; his cousin ED Morgan and C Oliver Iselin. It had originally been intended for *Columbia* to be refitted and upgraded as a trial horse for

Constitution, and it was for this purpose that ED Morgan had engaged Barr. Backed by these three and Nat Herreshoff in 1899, Barr had proved his worth. Still, whether he would win again in 1901 would not depend entirely on him or his crew: the outlook, involvement and the decisions of the syndicate of men who had created her were just as important. In contrast, though he had his captain and his manager to whom he delegated responsibility, Tommy was the sole owner. He represented the Royal Ulster Yacht Club, but it laid few if any constraints upon his decision-making powers. Each challenge was shaped in his image and he could do as he pleased.

Although it was more difficult for the Americans to stamp their individuality on the cup challenge, a look at one backer, J Pierpont Morgan, shows an interesting personality difference between him and Lipton. Morgan, born and educated in Hartford, Connecticut, and son of Junius, a very successful merchant banker in his own right, had started his own banking business in 1861. In the five decades that followed, he rose to a position of great power and influence, building a reputation as a supreme dealmaker who had funded the expansion of the steel industry and brokered the Great Railroad Treaty of 1865. By the time of Tommy's first challenge in 1899 J Pierpont Morgan was unquestionably one of the most powerful men in the world. To Morgan are attributed two pompous statements about yachting, namely, 'You can do business with anyone but you can only sail a boat with a gentleman' and 'Anyone who asks about the cost of maintaining a yacht shouldn't buy one.' With one-liners such as these it is not too difficult to see why Sir Thomas Lipton commanded such popular affection for his style in America's Cup endeavours. Tommy was also an open book compared to this complex man who preferred to pull the strings in secrecy, often conducting difficult negotiations on board one of his yachts.

Even so, the two men did have a regard for one another. Pierpont, who had been a pivotal figure in the Dunraven episodes, appreciated Lipton's conduct after the 1899 defeat. He also valued the fact that Tommy should follow up that defeat by presenting the New York Yacht Club with the $1,000 Lipton Cup in 1900, a challenge trophy for 70-foot yachts. Pierpont was also not oblivious to the fact that Tommy's personality broke down social barriers that his could not.

A marvellous story set at a dinner party on board the kaiser's imperial yacht is told by a former archduke named Leopold Wolfling. It was some years after Tommy's first America's Cup challenges and both Tommy and Morgan were there. Kaiser Wilhelm was in very bad humour and, Wolfling says, Morgan became frigid too. Tommy, however, just kept going with good humour and anecdotes about his boyhood struggles until the kaiser was rocking with laughter.

When the New York Yacht Club hosted a reception for 500 people in honour of Morgan and his outstanding service to the club in January 1901, Tommy sent a congratulatory telegram. Given that Tommy had challenged for the cup again, it was no surprise that Morgan in his speech should refer to his great adversary. Pointing to the America's Cup on the table in front of him he asked his guests, 'Is the confidence of this noble opponent justified? Will he, as he tritely put it, "Lift the Cup"?' As the room resounded with 'No', Morgan told his audience that if Sir Thomas did win he would deserve his success. 'And there is this consolation if he succeeds in his laudable ambition, America never could lose to a finer gentleman nor a more truly great sportsman.' Tommy had challenged America a second time and this was America's response.

In January 1901 Queen Victoria had died at Osborne House on the

Isle of Wight. Tommy's friend Edward, Prince of Wales, was crowned king. In March 1901 King Edward VII made Tommy a knight commander of the Victorian Order. On 6 September 1901 President William McKinley was shot twice in the stomach by a demented anarchist named Czolgosz at an exhibition in Buffalo; he died eight days later. In South Africa the Treaty of Vereeniging and the end of the Boer War was still eight months away, but there was common knowledge of the British camps there, in which more than 130,000 Boers were imprisoned in inhumane conditions, with thousands dying from disease. It had, then, already been a year of shocks and surprises, and on the stage of world events the America's Cup was not important at all. Yet it was so eagerly anticipated on both sides of the Atlantic that it became both a welcome distraction and the potential source of a needed boost to national morale. For the British in particular, a Lipton victory could not have been better timed.

Arguably, the biggest shock of the 1901 America's Cup itself took place before the starting gun was even fired. On 9 September Tommy entertained J Pierpont Morgan and two of his associates on his yacht, *Erin*, before taking them across to *Shamrock II*, where they were allowed a complete tour. Referring later to this extraordinary gesture Tommy simply said, 'It is only an incident in the era of good-feeling between the two nations.' But American yachting expert JR Spears saw it in history-making terms: 'This visit of Mr Morgan and friend to the *Shamrock* may be said to mark an era in the international races, for never before did anyone connected with either challenger or defender have opportunity to inspect his opponent before the races were held.'

After an appropriate period of delay following the death of the president, racing began in earnest on 27 September. Barr wasted no time in the pre-start manoeuvres. *Columbia* hounded *Shamrock II*, employing aggressive crowding tactics and incensing Sycamore. After his first foray into the arena with Barr he could hardly contain himself: 'If he is going to continue those tactics there will be serious trouble. What he did yesterday would not be tolerated in British waters. He must not expect us to stand for it and we won't.' That outburst came even after a night's sleep and a race that in the end was aborted because the time limit had been exceeded, but Barr had had the upper hand. Prior to the races Sycamore had predicted that 'any advantage gainable at the start would be of the utmost importance', and he was right: when the race was declared void *Columbia* had had a lead of over a mile, and was between 4 and 5 miles from the finishing mark.

Lipton did not protest. As the September visit of J Pierpont Morgan clearly demonstrates, he was too close to the Americans and arguably too much in awe of them ever to stir up a controversy. It was not his way. He would not stoop, as he saw it, to name-calling or using any other psychological battle tactics to unnerve the defenders. He simply stated that he had every confidence in Captain Sycamore and his crew, and he couldn't resist an additional, 'I must say I never saw a boat better handled than *Columbia*.' However, it had not been an auspicious pre-start or start to the *Shamrock II* campaign.

Saturday, 28 September 1901. For half an hour before the preparatory signal at 10.45 a.m. the two white-sheeted gladiators twisted and turned around one another, Barr's predatory instincts on display. But when the warning gun was fired at 10.50 it was Sycamore who had secured the windward side, outmanoeuvring Barr. He held this position as the 11 o'clock gun announced the start of the race. Still, he only led *Columbia* across the line by half a length. Both immediately went on to the port tack, heading south by east.

Mainsails, club topsails, jibs and foresails were all flying as Sycamore pushed *Shamrock II* into a 150-yard lead after a quarter of an hour. In a choppy sea, Barr closed the gap, pointing *Columbia* nearer to the wind. At 11.25 and just two boat lengths behind, he swung *Columbia* round on to the starboard tack. Sycamore did the same within a minute. Barr's tactic did not yield him any real advantage and after a further half hour he turned again on to the port tack.

By 1 o'clock the challenger and the defender were within 3 miles of the windward mark, the turning point, with less than 100 yards between them. Each drove their yacht as hard as they could to be first to the mark. Behind them was a widely spread fleet of excursion boats carrying a staggering 150,000 spectators. This was the drama at sea the watchers had all been hoping for.

Shamrock II and *Columbia* drew closer together. Closer. The mark was no longer distant and small, but near and large. Surely they were going to collide? But no, *Shamrock II* was ahead. She almost heeled over as she turned, crept round the mark and then surged forward once more, *Columbia* barely 40 seconds behind her at the mark. Spinnakers spread to starboard, balloon jibs broken out, these two billowing white giants raced for home, down the slope to the finish.

Shamrock II held her lead, but she needed every second to offset her time handicap. It was going to be a famous victory if she could only extend her advantage. Tommy watched from *Erin* through his binoculars, surrounded as always by chattering guests. *Shamrock II* was skimming more, cutting less. Watson had done his job well, and Sycamore and Jameson and the predominantly Brightlingsea crew were delivering.

By 2 o'clock the wind softened. The invisible bellows behind the sails were clapped out, nothing left to give. The stretched sails now flapped. No doubt about it, *Shamrock II* was surrendering her lead as

65

Columbia gained, closing the gap. And now she was passing the hapless, luckless *Shamrock II*. Distant cheers from the jubilant partisan flotilla could be heard above the slow slapping of the waves. By 2.30 *Columbia* was three lengths in front.

Half an hour to the finish and *Shamrock II* catapulted forward once more as Sycamore squeezed every last knot of speed from her. *Columbia* responded: Barr, the skipper's skipper, would not allow any lapse of concentration, especially now. A gentle breeze carried *Columbia* across the finish line just four lengths ahead of the challenger, a mere 37 seconds' difference. It had seemed close on the day, but the margin of victory was much greater when *Shamrock II*'s handicap, incurred due to a greater sail area, was taken into account: *Columbia*'s margin of victory was officially measured as 1 minute and 20 seconds.

Tommy declared that *Shamrock II* was beaten fair and square, but he bemoaned the lack of wind: 'We want a breeze that will put the deck of *Shamrock* 6 inches under water. Then you will see a race. She was fairly licked today.'

Two days later, with *Shamrock II* leading in a lazy, drifting match, the time limit was once more the winner and the race was abandoned. The 3 October duel was different again, raced on a triangular course. Barr stalked his opponent as a top athlete runs on the shoulder of a pacesetter. Sycamore guided *Shamrock II* into a lead to windward and to leeward, with *Columbia* never far behind. Barr was, if not content to follow, then at least comfortable, always within striking distance. As they turned for the final leg, almost to the sound of an invisible bell, the defender seemed to accelerate. Barr held Sycamore to leeward, pointing *Columbia* higher and nearer to the wind, and it was only a matter of minutes before she had left *Shamrock II* in her wake. The outcome of the race was no longer in much doubt.

Nevertheless, this duel wasn't yet a foregone conclusion. *Shamrock II* was competitive, and Charlie Barr, though confident, was cautious not to be complacent at any stage of any match. The next and potentially deciding match was scheduled for the next day. No time for Sycamore to dwell on mistakes or what might have been, he still had time to make amends.

On 4 October *Columbia* made the more impressive start, making better judgement on tacks to both port and starboard, rebuilding speed and momentum to attack the start line just before the gun sounded. *Shamrock II* charged behind her. Less than 20 minutes into this two-leg course she passed the defender; she wasn't finished yet. Passing the mark, *Shamrock II* had less than a minute's advantage over *Columbia*. Her spinnaker dropped in the water, but the heavy sodden sail was gathered in quickly enough; failure to have done so would have spelled disaster. As it was, Sycamore held the lead. *Columbia* chased relentlessly, waiting for a mistake, looking for a weakness, a bad decision. Sycamore had to keep Barr in check.

Is it possible, as America's Cup historian John Rousmaniere has pointed out, that Sycamore and his afterguard were fearful of Charlie Barr's well-trained crew and were 'unwilling to tack on her opponent's wind and thus start a tacking duel?' Was that the defining moment, when Sycamore lacked the aggression and the killer distinct to cut off his opponent? Or did he lack confidence in his own crew's ability to react quickly enough in close combat? Certainly, Sycamore was more consultative with his afterguard than Barr, and he didn't have that instantaneous decision-making authority of the wily Scot.

In the event, both boats tacked again and again in the quest for clear air, an uplift of breeze and tactical advantage. They zigzagged across the course, crossing close to one another again at 3.20. In a final dash for the line both yachts luffed, pointing their bows into the wind, making the sails flutter. *Shamrock II* was first to the line. She had beaten *Columbia* by just 2 seconds. Or had she? First across the line, but defeated by the time added on for her sail area. It was a spirited performance and at last there was something to cheer about, even though the thrill of finishing first was short-lived.

The simple fact remained, however, that a new, improved and faster *Shamrock II* could not outperform a yacht Herreshoff had designed for the 1899 defence. Much was made by Tommy, and subsequent, mainly British, commentators, of the fact that over a total of distance of 90 miles *Shamrock II* lost to *Columbia* by an aggregate of only 3 minutes and 27 seconds in actual time. However, *Shamrock II* was still beaten, outclassed by *Columbia*. However hard Captain Sycamore and his afterguard tried to counter and attack *Columbia*, and arguably they were not aggressive enough, they could not match her for speed. Nor was *Shamrock II*'s crew as adept or responsive as Barr's experienced, well-drilled team.

Even years later, when speaking of *Shamrock II* in his autobiography, Tommy makes the marvellously understated comment, 'she was just a shade too slow'. It is hard to believe that his memory was so rose-tinted. He goes on, 'What splendid racing we had that year. I really think that with the slightest shade of luck I might have pulled off a victory.' Tommy only seemed, or wanted, to remember the fact that *Shamrock II* had been complimented by all knowledgeable yachtsmen as 'the best and swiftest challenger ever sent over', and that this *Shamrock* had physically crossed the line ahead of Columbia in one race. 'That was a sporting finish if ever there was one', Tommy recalled.

He shows no anger or pent-up frustration, no desire to scapegoat and no tendency towards retrospective 'if only's in his recollections. Of course, from a cynical perspective it is easy to say for a second time that victory would have been an unexpected bonus for him, that, in truth, he had succeeded in scoring another notable public relations coup for his business. But there is not a word, not a single word from his lips or pen or in his reports to his company directors or his shareholders, ten, twenty or thirty years later, that suggests he was in the America's Cup just to sell more tea or expand his business interests in the United States. No doubt it was a welcome part of the mix, but only that. His America's Cup challenges were never measured by business profit.

His rose-tinted attitude to defeat had its origins in his own self-confidence, his entrepreneurial spirit and his insatiable desire to nurture a special relationship between Britain and America. He had satisfied himself that he had delegated the key tasks of design, management and sailing as well as he could. He knew, too, that he had spared no expense and had given the whole endeavour as much of his personal attention as it was possible to give. Most importantly, he had now fully restored the America's Cup to the status of 'contest between friendly nations' and reduced the tension in Anglo-American relations in a way that was unimaginable for any British diplomat. That in itself was a remarkable achievement.

And, as much as any of these considerations, what mattered to Tommy was the sense of having repaid his debt to his royal patron, Edward. This was now, after all, a more uncertain world, with no Queen Victoria, an assassinated American president and a rapidly expanding industrial America pouring scorn on the hypocrisy and greed of British military adventures in South Africa. Tommy's whole demeanour, his humble origins and distance from the British establishment, his Irish Scottishness and, not least, his natural affinity with Americans were all attractive qualities, and neither the king nor his grocer were blind to the extraordinary amount of goodwill the latter was creating.

As for a third challenge, there was little doubt that Tommy would try again; a shamrock has three leaves, he liked to say. He would definitely be back because his challenges, and the blend of business skills, charm, common touch, media savvy and diplomacy he brought to them allowed him to occupy a space in between business, celebrity, diplomacy, sport and international sportsmanship, a space no one had occupied before and where no one – not a Morgan, nor a Barr, nor even a king – could join him. In this sense he did use the America's Cup to his own ends, as showcase for his dazzling array of skills – skills that he had developed and refined on his rise from grocer to global entrepreneur.

4

Grocer to global entrepreneur

Intrepid tourists travelling by train across Egypt in the mid 1880s were reminded of just how far Tommy Lipton had come since he opened his first grocery store in Glasgow in 1871. From Alexandra, they made their way though the Nile Delta, accompanied by plagues of flies, and on to Cairo. These fearless nineteenth-century sightseers then made the short journey to the legendary Sphinx and, beyond it, the Great Pyramid of Cheops. The tombs and treasures of King Cheops in this, the largest of the great pyramids at Giza, had long since been plundered and it would be another thirty years before the breathtaking discoveries of Howard Carter in the Valley of the Kings.

Undeterred by their 450-foot ascent of the Great Pyramid, these indefatigable visitors set upon the less daunting but still challenging nearby Pyramid of Cephrenes. On their descent they noticed where stones had been removed and an entrance exposed. The arched stones above the passage were huge and one displayed hieroglyphic writing.

But another, just as large and as prominent, exhibited a message that clearly was not the work of the ancient stone carvers. On this stone was written 'Lipton Scotland'. Questioning of the Arab guides drew the response that Mr Lipton was indeed a very good man, who had given the Arabs on hand 'plenty handsome backsheesh' for their craftwork. Spontaneous and opportunistic as ever, Tommy had been more than happy to pay for this monumental advertisement.

This extraordinary tale featured in the *Glasgow Herald* on 11 January 1886. It would not have surprised Scottish readers familiar with Lipton, his rapidly expanding business and his endlessly innovative approaches to advertising. Asked repeatedly about the secrets of his success in the grocery business in the 1880s and 1890s, Tommy often cited hard work and honest dealing with customers and suppliers alike. However, he never left out advertising, for he knew as well as anyone what a vital element it was in elevating him from Glasgow grocer to global entrepreneur.

It was often said in the mountains of press coverage about him that Tommy never forgot his humble origins. He certainly adored his parents, in death as well as life, and he had gained his first working and sales experience in their grocery store as a young teenager. As we have seen, he was also employed for a short while in a Glasgow stationery shop and a shirtmaker's after leaving school to supplement the family's income. While this gives plenty proof of his humble origins, there is nothing in these experiences, or in any others of his known early life in Glasgow, that can explain Tommy's innovative approach to advertising from the outset. The only plausible explanation is his experiences in America, most especially those weeks spent in the New York grocery store.

So, when Tommy opened his first grocery store in Glasgow he

aspired to much more than eking out a meagre living like his parents. They, though honest, hard-working folk, were not at all entrepreneurial in spirit. In fact, they were concerned, when their son embarked on this enterprise, that people would think the Liptons were getting above themselves.

Tommy, on the other hand, was bursting with ideas, but even in his wild enthusiasm he carefully considered every aspect of his business, particularly the competition, and, most importantly, his potential customers. He would have readily agreed with the assertion of the great management thinker and author Peter Drucker, born some sixty years later, that the only valid definition of business purpose is to create a customer.

From day one, on 10 May 1871, Lipton's Market at 101 Stobcross Street was outstanding. The hunger of Glasgow's working classes for a wider range of affordable foods, though great indeed, was nothing compared to Tommy's ambition and hunger for success. Tommy knew that the site of this first shop had previously been a grocer's but had remained unoccupied for the previous five years. He also knew that the staple diet of working-class people did not include ham, cheese and eggs but comprised instead of potatoes, salt herring and a rough, dry bread. Dairy products were something of a luxury and normally beyond the weekly budget of working people, many of whom were earning less than £2 a week. It may have been the heyday of the British Empire, especially for the pioneering engineering and shipbuilding city of Glasgow, but the average wage for a Scottish worker in the period of Lipton's commercial birth was between £70 and £80 per annum. And it was this urban labour market in a quickly overcrowding city of 477,000 souls that was Tommy's target market.

In comparison, thanks to his American adventure, Tommy was

already a wealthy man, having at his disposal £100 to put into his new business. With this he acquired the lease of the shop for a small fee and set about transforming it. In the north side of the city, close to the river at Lancefield Quay, Stobcross Street was ideally situated for the delivery of supplies and for passing trade. It was a busy, thriving part of the city – one that was coated in grime from industrial chimneys coughing up their soot and smoke.

The first part of Tommy's strategy for success was to differentiate his Stobcross shop from all the others, which tended to be unadventurous. Visual presentation and vivacious sales staff were about as low down the list of priorities as it was possible to be, and shopping was not, in any modern sense, an experience: it was about the provision of the essentials of life as cheaply and with as little fuss as possible. When Tommy opened up for business it was May and therefore light in the evenings, so the workers on the Clyde and in the factories who made their way home past the shopfronts of Stobcross had to wait until the winter months to see the full effect of Tommy's first innovation: his brightly lit windows. They would, however, have discerned a difference straight away: most storefronts were not eyecatching at any time of year, but Tommy had cleaned, painted and decorated his new store inside and out, and the sign above the shop entrance was big and bold: LIPTON'S MARKET.

Tommy himself was a key part of his 'marketing mix'. Rising early, he was always first to meet the boats coming in from Ireland, loading up his cart with the pick of fresh hams, cheeses, eggs and butter. Dressed smartly in a spotless white apron, he'd then spend the day at the shop. Sometimes he would be outside cleaning his windows and talking to complete strangers. Quick with a laugh and a joke, he was cordial with customers, but not pushy. Of course, he always charmed his way into conversations about his special offers.

Not only that, Tommy also had his product strategy just right: his wares were of good quality, and he had secured his lines of supply, principally with Ireland, though he also bought produce off the steamers that regularly docked on the Clyde. His product was secured because he made a point of paying cash up front, so as his demand increased suppliers trusted him all the more and recognised that it was in their own interests to supply Lipton with the best quality.

The price component of the 'marketing mix' was undoubtedly winning over customers as well. Although Tommy took just £2 6s from his first day's trading at Stobcross Street, that was still much more than an average single day's taking in his parents' grocery store in the Gorbals. Going to Lipton's quickly became a habit for many ordinary working-class people, and the one-man manager, shop assistant, salesman, cashier, errand boy and home-delivery service was working flat out.

Tommy had the ideal strategy to ensure a better living than his parents had ever gained from their corner grocery store. His father, who lacked any ambition, would no doubt have been satisfied with the Stobcross Street success, perhaps even circumspect about the merits of expanding. However, Tommy was powered by an ambitious self-belief that few, if any, of his high street competitors could match. Yet, always careful in his preparation and meticulous in his planning, he wasn't in a hurry to expand, concentrating on his first shop. In fact, a full four years would elapse between the opening of the first and second shops.

Tommy's ambition was driven, in part, by a desire to be better known, to be famous. He was more than ready to massage the truth when it suited his purpose, and his quest to be talked about was just as audacious. From personally giving out handbills in the street to a tentative attempt at newspaper advertising – the first of which cost Tommy 7s 6d, he claimed – to the hanging of a painted wooden ham outside his shop, Tommy was relentless in his pursuit of promotion. His real breakthrough, however, was the idea to engage the services of a gifted cartoonist by the name of William Lockhart.

Tommy's scheme was simple: Willie would sketch an amusing cartoon that would be displayed in the shop window on the Monday morning. It would then remain there for the week, attracting more and more people each day. It was more than something to look at, it was something to laugh at, and it was not lost on Tommy that an entertained potential customer was more likely to become a purchasing customer.

One cartoon, with the caption 'Going to Lipton's' showed a line of gaunt, pencil-thin figures walking into a shop. Adjacent to it was another illustration, this time of a line of healthy and very rotund figures 'Coming from Lipton's'. Another pictured a rather overweight man travelling with a very thin man in the last compartment of a train. The rotund gentleman says to his fellow traveller, 'Are you not afraid to travel in the collision department?' only to receive answer, 'Oh no, not so long as I have a Lipton buffer opposite.' Lockhart's early cartoons for Tommy also featured pigs, developing the concept of them as Lipton's orphans. An Irishman is carrying a sack on his back. He meets another who asks, 'What's the matter with the pig, Pat?' To which the reply was, 'Sure, sorr, he's an orphan, so out of pity I'm taking him to Lipton.'

Willie Lockhart's creativity knew no bounds. It is difficult to exaggerate the impact of his cartoons and his other handiwork on the public and, therefore, on Tommy Lipton's reputation and business. Lockhart's other handiwork included the art of butter sculpture and, even more extraordinary, figures carved out of sausage and cheese. Although hardly sophisticated by modern marketing standards, his food sculptures made the storefront of Lipton's Market stand out from those of all his competitors. Over the years he remained keen to be innovative – much later he even installed concave mirrors at the entrance of his store that made customers seem thin and gaunt; as they left, they were faced with convex mirrors that rendered them fat and jolly. The very idea of using humour and laughter as a means of not only attracting but also retaining customers was novel indeed.

Yet Tommy was only just getting into his stride. His most comical or even outrageous advertising ploy was to bring one of Lockhart's cartoons to life, taking the theatre of his store into the street.

In order to achieve this, Tommy recruited any young man he could find and persuaded him, with the prospect of generous payment, to dress up in a spurious all-green Irish national costume and lead a group of pigs from the Livestock Market to Lipton's. Tied to the pigs' flanks was the message 'The Orphans, Home-fed, Bound for Lipton's'. As if that wasn't enough, Tommy instructed his mock-Irish swineherds to lie down and take a nap at a public and busy crossroads, thereby causing a disturbance and something of a nuisance, especially for horse-driven carts. Police and local traders were not amused, but the public loved the stunt. It caused hilarity in the streets, and needless to say the ploy was used up to the 1890s all over Britain when new shops were opening.

Throughout the 1870s and a good part of the 1880s, ideas were coming out of Tommy almost as fast as ham and eggs were being carried out of his shops. Another wheeze, or infamous Lipton stunt as far as the forces of the law were concerned, was the distribution, in 1877, of Lipton-ised imitation bank notes. Given out as handbills, these exactly matched in colour and size the pound notes of the National Bank of Scotland. By this time, Tommy had several stores in the

Glasgow area, and he had the addresses of his High Street and Paisley stores printed on the notes in small lettering. The name of LIPTON'S was also featured, as well as the statement that 1 pound's worth of great Irish ham, butter and eggs would be given for only 15 shillings.

Soon, unscrupulous behaviour led to these notes being passed off as legal tender. Chaos ensued, with Lipton being branded an outrage and a fraud. The Scottish newspapers in April 1877 carried endless stories about the imitation notes, including an ultimately unsuccessful lawsuit against Mr Lipton raised by Francis McConnell, a clerk of Cathcart Road. Sheriff Lees at the Sheriff Small Debt Court in Glasgow dismissed the case as incompetent, the inference being that Mr McConnell wasn't much of a clerk if he couldn't tell the difference between a real bank note and one with words like 'Lipton's' and 'ham and eggs' on it. Even so, Tommy withdrew the notes from circulation as quickly as possible to avoid any further confusion or retribution. He had, anyway, already achieved his objective.

Cartoons, butter sculptures, funny mirrors, roaming pigs, imitation bank notes – what next? In 1881 Tommy could reflect on ten years of high street trading with considerable satisfaction. His intuitive marketing skills had paid off handsomely, and his reputation for imaginitively advertised quality foodstuffs sold at the fairest of prices was secured.

From Stobcross Street he had gone on to open a second shop about a mile away in the High Street of Glasgow. Another followed in Govan, then Jamaica Street, a principal thoroughfare of the city. Stores in the area surrounding Glasgow were also soon trading, in places like Paisley and Greenock, further down the Clyde. In the build-up to each new shop opening, handbills were widely distributed, newspaper advertisements ran and posters advertised simply 'Lipton is coming'. Tommy always made a point of being present at each shop opening, exuding charm and bonhomie, drawing attention to the special offers and serving at least the first half dozen customers himself. It was a potent experience for ordinary working-class people, one for which even the local press and word-of-mouth advertising would not have prepared them for.

Approaching the store from the opposite end of the street on the eve of its opening, timed to coincide with payday, they would most likely have seen crowds of people huddled around the brightly lit window display of cartoons of pigs, hens, ducks and, of course, the roly-poly and scraggy men, beneath the giant sign of LIPTON'S MARKET. On entering the shop, their senses would have been overwhelmed by the competing aromas of assorted cheeses and cured hams. Lining the walls, from floor to ceiling, behind the horseshoe counter whose curved contour dominated the whole interior of the store, would have been rows of hams. Bacon, butter and cheeses such as Dunlop, Cheddar and Stilton would have been arranged in various displays. Between ten and fifteen sales staff in white aprons stood on spotlessly scrubbed floors, flanked by up to three cash boys, all ready to serve. All that was available to tempt the customer was clearly visible, not least because each store was well illuminated, with up to sixty gas jets burning brightly within opal globes. What a joy, then, for the curious new customer that the prices did not reflect the ostentatious presentation of the produce.

By the time Tommy was ready to expand beyond his native West of Scotland he was a local retailing phenomenon. His next port of call was Dundee. The opening of the Dundee store in 1878 was a shrewd choice as the city had been booming since the 1840s, thanks in large part to the international demand for jute. One jute factory alone, run by Cox Brothers, employed 14,000 people, just the sort of working-class people that were Tommy's target market. However, Tommy's own account of his reasons for going to Dundee typifies his extraordinary shamelessness in spinning a cock-and-bull story. Tommy had engaged a certain Herr Schultz to teach him German. Herr Schultz had apparently been paid in advance by the munificent Mr Lipton and then failed to deliver the lessons. The enraged Mr Lipton had visited Herr Schultz, becoming Lipton the pugilist. The fugitive Mr Lipton had then outwitted the Glasgow police and fled to Dundee, where he saw the potential for a store.

There is probably some small grain of truth in this story, but no more than a grain. One possible explanation for Tommy's habit of telling tall tales such as this is that he was always at pains to avoid any public perception of him as a hardheaded, calculating and profit-making businessman. To be successful in the business of delivering quality foods for, predominantly, the working classes at affordable prices, he had to be a man of the people. Another justification for his putting one part truth and seven parts nonsense into his anecdotes is his deliberate romanticising of his business. Once he had started the antics he could not stop, and he would go to any length to keep the name of Tommy Lipton on everyone's lips. The first sign of failure would be when the man in the street, Tommy's bread and butter, stopped talking about him. Herr Schultz? A desire to learn German? Not a lie, just Tommy feeding his publicity machine.

It is interesting to note that in the run-up to the opening of the Dundee store Tommy started the first of more than one hundred giant coffee-table volumes of press cuttings that mentioned his name and his business. These became his life's record for he left no diary, no correspondence and no confessional memoir. The pseudo-autobiographical *Leaves from the Lipton Logs* reads, alas, like one long after-dinner speech.

In it Tommy more or less recalls his best stories, seasoned with added embellishments for good measure, and there is very little of any real substance in its pages. Nationals like the *Glasgow Herald*, *The Scotsman*, *The London Times* and even *The New York Times* are interspersed with the likes of the *American Dairyman*, the *Indian Planters Gazette* and *New Women* magazine, and with remarkable honesty, Tommy kept everything – even the uncomplimentary and the unsavoury.

The press notices about his Dundee store also serve to illustrate just how well Tommy was doing after seven years in business. His two-day Easter sale, starting on Good Friday the year after, had the local press in Dundee salivating over Mr Lipton's stock of 25,000 hams, 100,000 pounds of bacon, 22,400 pounds of butter and 250,000 eggs. The sale stock had vanished by the time Easter Sunday dawned. In short, Tommy was now receiving publicity for the sheer scale of his operation and new Lipton's Markets were appearing with increasing regularity across Scotland.

As the number of stores grew so did Tommy's business interests, and his need to ensure constancy and quality in supply to meet the exploding demand took him back to the United States in 1880. After visiting New York, Philadelphia and Cincinnati he settled on Chicago, acquiring a meat packing facility. Although it had the capacity to dispatch 400 pigs a day, it would be another five years before it became fully functional and still longer before it reached its full potential.

Cheese was also on his mind on that American trip of 1880, but this time it wasn't just a question of finding new suppliers. Nor was it just about 'differentiation', as a modern business strategist might describe it, or the adoption an alternative strategy from competitors in order to keeping ahead of them. Tommy's concerns even went beyond what author and *Financial Times* journalist John Kay has more recently described as the three primary sources of distinctive business capability: namely architecture (the pattern of supplier and customer relationships), reputation and innovation. In his nine years f trading, Tommy had been attentive to all of these.

But what helped to make him so successful was his innate understanding that these aspects were interdependent, as well as his skill in anticipating when the business would need fresh impetus. He didn't think 'this bit is marketing' or 'this meeting is operations' or 'this is finance' – he saw the business as a whole. Put more simply, he sought to kill more than two birds with one stone in every business activity and initiative. And he always picked up the pace before customers, suppliers and the media grew tired of the Lipton offering.

So, in 1880 and 1881 when Tommy secured supplies of cheese direct from America he was introducing a broader range of products into his stores and reducing his dependence on Irish dairy suppliers, for whom he had had some strong words in recent years regarding the tendency of Irish farmers to stockpile butter for up to six months before making it available for sale. Though genial and ready to orchestrate comic stunts, he was by no means complaisant when it came to his industry. He cared about it and its quality. However, that in itself wouldn't get people talking or make news. An examination of his press clippings from this period – from *The Scotsman* to the *Yorkshire Post* to the *Boston Herald* – shows that he came up with the ideal solution in the form of a truly inspired marketing ploy.

On 8 December 1882 the Anchor Line steamer *Bolivia* docked on the River Clyde. For the second year in a row, it carried a remarkable cargo: three cheeses, the product of a herd of 800 cows belonging to Dr Wight of Whitesboro, New York. Each cheese measured 5 feet in diameter, was 2 feet 2 inches wide and 16 feet in circumference.

One weighed 2,400 pounds, the other two were 2,100 pounds each.

These jumbo cheeses, as they became known, went beyond the absurd. In the name of commerce, they were led through the streets followed by cheering crowds to be exhibited in three Lipton's Markets: Glasgow, Edinburgh and the first English store, Leeds, opened in 1881. The spectacle of watching them being manhandled by teams of men through the narrow doorways of Lipton's stores was the greatest attraction. Scheduled to be cut up on Christmas Eve, they succeeded in drawing both crowds and the press, and the ploy worked so well that by 1885 Tommy was arranging for twelve cheeses to be made, each one weighing in at 4,000 pounds.

The longevity of the jumbo cheese era is more understandable when it is taken into account that in this period Tommy was conquering new cities and creating thousands of new customers. He opened in Liverpool in 1883 and in Manchester and Sunderland in 1885. Cardiff followed in 1887, Swansea and Belfast in 1889. No doubt with an eye on publicity for the all-important first London store, Tommy wrote to Queen Victoria in March 1887, offering to present to her a cheese that would weigh a staggering 11,200 pounds, or not less than 5 tons. Quite how long it would have taken Queen Victoria and the extended royal families across Europe to consume such a cheese has not been calculated. Disappointingly, Sir Henry Ponsonby replied that Her Majesty could not possibly receive any presents for her Jubilee from individuals with whom she was not personally acquainted. The missed opportunity grated with Tommy.

In 1888 the first Lipton's Market in London did open, with the usual fanfare. Important though this was to him and the business, Tommy didn't need the breakthrough in London to make his fortune: he was already a millionaire with multiple retail outlets in the major urban centres across Britain.

His days of donning a white apron, polishing his windows and even sleeping under his own counter were now a distant memory. The business was sustainable and had shown spectacular year-on-year growth, but this also meant that each year the distances between genial, creative, energetic Tommy and his market stores became greater and greater. It is interesting, in this light, to consider his hiring policy. In the early years he simply hired men he liked the look of to manage his stores. He asked what their current pay was and offered more or double. This was how he recruited William Love, one of his first employees, who was to become a trusted manager and friend for many years. Other early employees, boys mainly, took Tommy's first advance payment and never returned to work.

Though there has been speculation in more recent years about the extraordinarily close relationship Tommy had with William Love in particular, and later with others such as his private secretary, Joe Slade, it is very unlikely that the strong personal and emotional attachment spilled over into a physical relationship of any kind. Tommy was too astute, too mindful of the consequences, the public disgrace and the collapse of his business. Imagine the ire of his principal suppliers in Ireland, or the dim view his Catholic customers would have taken, or, for that matter, the reaction of Presbyterian Scotland as a whole. The reaction of his mother to any such revelation doesn't even bear thinking about; it would have resulted in humiliation and possibly complete separation, which was much more than Tommy could have borne.

Tommy did not seek a political career, as he made clear to one journalist in the 1880s, but he did aspire to a public life. The very way he went about his business, in contrast to most of his competitors, made him a public figure. He lived in the newspapers. Emotionally and commercially he could not have coped with even the slightest hint of a public insinuation of what at the time would have been widely perceived as a most inappropriate liaison. So much of who he was and the success of his business centred on trust, openness and his ability to relate to others. People turning their back on him because of what they thought he might be – homosexual – would have been too much to bear. Certainly, the media then was not nearly as intrusive as it is today and the odds were against such a story being brought to public attention. However, it was always in Tommy's interests to keep any male relationships literally and euphemistically at arm's length.

Such speculation should not be allowed to obscure the fact that over many years Tommy inspired a number of loyal and trusted lieutenants in his business. Whatever else William Love might have been, he was a conscientious and hardworking general manager, and later director, who modelled himself on Lipton both in his appearance and work ethic. Moreover, once Tommy had worked out the correct timing of his financial incentives for other important but less pivotal employees, such as the store men and cash boys, he held on to them for longer periods, proving to be a good and fair employer, and schooling all in his particular style of customer relations and soft-selling. It was certainly not a question of public gent, private tyrant.

In 1886 Tommy initiated what was to be called an 'annual conversazione'. Rather than being an exercise in team building, or even an opportunity for staff to quiz the owner of the business and the senior managers, it was intended to promote that much sought-after modern corporate virtue, a sense of identity and loyalty among employees. Tommy could not be present for the scheduled March date of the first conversazione, in Glasgow's Bath Street, but he did attend one, less than one year later.

This conversazione, for as many of his employees as could attend, amounting to some two hundred men and women, took place at the Assembly Rooms, again in Bath Street, on Wednesday, 26 January 1887. A buff pink pocket-sized fold-over card advertised the programme as commencing at 8 o'clock prompt. The evening began with the warm and witty Chairman's Address, followed by three songs sung by a lady and a gentleman, for which the assembled company would have sat and listened attentively.

The programme then dictated that eight dances would follow – a triumph, a quadrille, a schottische, a waltz, a polka, a lancers, a petronella and a waltz to finish – with an interlude for a solo dance of a 'Sailor's Hornpipe' in the middle of them. All this was more than enough exertion to build up an appetite for meats and cheeses and, of course, a cup of specially blended Lipton's tea.

Tommy himself was in sparkling form. His ability to mix and mingle with ease was partly an innate gift and partly a consequence of his experience in working his way up literally from the shop floor. He was as relaxed talking to clerks, secretaries, delivery men and store men as to directors. On this particular occasion in 1887 he enjoyed joking about how many jumbo cheeses it would take to make a stack as high as Nelson's Column.

In his address Tommy gave his staff the example of the French soldier who carried the baton of a marshal in his knapsack, thus indicating that every private, by attention to duty and being mindful of his own aspirations, could rise to the highest rank. The same principle applied in Lipton's: advancement by merit is our motto, he told them. He had to offer only three words of advice, namely cleanliness, civility and equality. By equality, he continued, he meant that equal attention should be shown to rich and poor alike. To warm applause, Tommy completed this mission statement of corporate responsibility by stating that the poor man's 20 shillings was as good as the rich man's pound.

The decade ended with a surge of store openings in London between 1888 and 1890 – Westbourne Grove, Clapham Junction, Lambeth Walk, Westminster, Islington et al – while the chain across the country was ever lengthening. There were now over a hundred and fifty Lipton's Markets nationwide, and the business was turning over in excess of £1 million. At least two to three stores were opening every month somewhere in Britain, but in each locale Tommy was careful to remember the early lessons of entertaining customers and making the store feel relevant to people's lives: the pigs paraded, the butter sculptures represented a local theme or landmark.

Up until this point Tommy had lived in the Cambuslang area of Glasgow with his parents and also his right-hand man William Love in what might seem an unusual cohabitation today, but one which did not seem inappropriate at the time. However, the death of his mother in 1889 and of his father in 1890 and rapid expansion of his businesses in London combined to precipitate the relocation of himself and his head office down south. He was never to live in Scotland again.

Tommy chose Osidge, a villa in Southgate, Hertfordshire, north of London, for his new home. It was situated just less than 10 miles from his new business headquarters at the City Road in London. It took some years to customise both Osidge and the expansive City Road site to Tommy's liking and needs, but these were to be his two bases for the rest of his life.

A gauge of the scale of Tommy's success was the increasing challenge of the annual conversazioni. In the space of a few short years his pay-roll had gone well into four figures and intimate evenings for a few hundred were no longer an option. It is characteristic of both the generosity and the affection-seeking nature of the man that he endeavoured to accommodate thousands at both Osidge and Theydon Bois, a park in Essex. As numbers mushroomed in the 1890s he created two separate all-day events, one for administrative and clerical staff and another for the more senior staff.

As we know, Tommy was not a man to lay on just tea and buns, and with each passing year the annual conversazione became a more extravagant affair. Special carriages were provided to transport staff from train stations. The day's events, which stretched on into the evening, comprised of musical performances, games, races, tea of course, Highland dancing and even pipe bands. It was not uncommon for the great and good to be invited to witness and partake in this social extravaganza.

Tommy's financial and enlightened commitment to these events is commendable. Not only do they illustrate his intuitive understanding that good relations with his workforce were a vital ingredient for loyalty, productivity and customer service, these bountiful conversazioni provide further proof, if any were needed, that Tommy did not do anything in half measures.

Apart from the vacuum left in his life by the death of his parents, Tommy had it all: wealth, success, a loyal workforce, a growing circle of influential acquaintances – rather than friends – and, perhaps most importantly, the commercial freedom to do whatever he chose. Even the *American Dairyman* had proclaimed in its pages that the ramifications of Mr Lipton's business reached 'from Denmark to Australia and from India to the Rocky Mountains'. And this was long before Tommy set foot in 1890 on the ship that was destined to deposit him in Ceylon, where his new life as a global tea trader would begin. With such success already in place, and with nothing to prove to anyone, why did Tommy become involved in a trade he knew nothing about and in which there were already established players? The answer is one that might be given by any entrepreneur: he saw the opportunity and the timing was right. And, moreover, he had the wherewithal and a ready-made network of distribution.

However, before even setting foot on Ceylon, Tommy had been of the belief that the drinking of tea had become more popular in Britain in the 1880s, having previously been regarded as a rather upper-class beverage and, at 3s 4d per pound, beyond the purse of the ordinary mortal. In fact, he asserted, he had been hounded by wholesalers to sell their tea – a lucrative deal indeed for any that were successful. This, he said, had prompted him to carry out his own research in London's Mincing Lane Market by Tower Hill. Mincing Lane was at that time a famous street market – not of the same pedigree of the nearby Leadenhall Market, which originated in the fourteenth century, was destroyed by the Great Fire of London in 1666 and has been reborn again and again – but important nonetheless for tea trading. Here, Tommy had ascertained the percentage of profit taken by the middlemen, and it was here that he had bought small quantities at auction in the first instance, or at least so he said.

This is, however, misleading. In fact, through his stores and agents Tommy actually sold 4 million pounds (weight) of tea in 1889. The following year he sold 6 million pounds. The reason for this high level of sales is that he had started to employ his own skilled tea blenders and, mindful of his own customer base, had slashed the price. Though the days of 3s 4d for a pound of tea were gone, most retailers were still sell-ing tea, mainly from China, for 2s 6d or half a crown. Tommy had stepped in with a quite unheard-of low price of 1s 7d for his blended tea. The cheap tea on offer in Lipton's Markets had attracted new cus-tomers and boasted overall sales.

Business became so big that he opened his own tea warehouse in Glasgow. He was undercutting high-street retailers in an established market and could not expect to go unchallenged, but was selling in excess of 30 tons a week by the end of 1889. Despite his theatrical down-playing of his knowledge of the tea market, it is still to Tommy's credit as businessman and entrepreneur that he saw the bigger picture, looking beyond Britain to see how he could dominate the tea market with his own brand by cutting out the middlemen and controlling the whole process from plantation to shop counter.

Interestingly, Ceylon wasn't the obvious choice for any aspiring global entrepreneur bent on domination of the tea market; the island was famed for its elephants, its cinnamon and other spices, its coffee even, but not its tea. China and India dominated the international mar-ket, with 70 per cent and 20 per cent respectively. In the previous hundred years the proud people of Ceylon had endured the ignominy of being ruled by the British and the Dutch, only to be handed over to the French. After several naval engagements and an attack on the coastal fort, the French had captured the eastern port of Trincomalee. The Treaty of Paris of 1783 that ended the American War of Independence also encompassed separate agreements between Britain, France, Spain and the Netherlands. This included a continuation of the earlier Dutch occupation of Ceylon. It was the British, however, who regained control of Ceylon at the end of the eighteenth century and transformed it into a plantation economy.

With its so-called Wet Zone to the south and west of the island, Ceylon had presented the ideal growing conditions for the coffee plant, at least until 1878 when a virulent coffee fungus destroyed much of their crop and with it the confidence of the markets. The story of tea on Ceylon only began in 1867 when another Scotsman, a James Taylor from Laurencekirk in Kincardineshire, planted the first seeds of a commercial tea plantation – a total of just 19 acres. Taylor was at that time the superintendent of the Loolecondera Estate. However, initially tea did not flourish as coffee had done because of a basic lack of expertise and difficulties in ensuring a supply of quality seed. The demise of the coffee plantations also led to fears of a similar blight for tea and the consequent financial losses.

Still, it had expanded sufficiently for there to be approaching 150,000 acres, not yet the size of 3 square miles, by the time Lipton surveyed the scene in May 1890. A decade later the total commercial tea acreage had risen to no less than 384,000 acres. However, not all of the overall transformation was attributable to Tommy Lipton. Capitalising on the low land prices the coffee blight had caused, Tommy bought several plantations in Ceylon, but these amounted to only 5,000 acres, a small percentage of the total acreage. Few at home would have believed this given the intensity of the branding and advertising that followed Lipton's new status as tea plantation owner. In fact, the Ceylon plantations delivered only a small proportion of his retail needs: most of his tea he bought from India. As Tommy well knew, the greater speed, efficiency and predictability of the steamships – in marked contrast to the tea clippers and other cargo ships that had dominated the nineteenth century – were transforming world trade and the consumption of commodities in Britain. More exotic products could be delivered cheaper, faster and with far greater reliability.

The first poster advertisements proclaimed:

LIPTON'S TEAS.
DIRECT FROM THE TEA GARDENS TO THE TEA POT.
NO MIDDLEMEN PROFITS TO PAY.
RICH, PURE AND FRAGRANT.
THE FINEST TEA THE WORLD CAN PRODUCE.

Underneath there was a sketch of a modest Ceylonese girl holding a cup with the words 'Lipton's Tea' emblazoned on it.

He made the whole concept of drinking tea exotic, romantic and, most importantly, affordable. Long before modern fair trade and ethical supply-line ideas, Tommy was reproducing photographs of the Ceylonese terraces where the tea originated, as well as of the workers and factories. These were placed inside the tea packets. Admittedly this had more to do with the authenticity and romanticism of the product, but it was nevertheless also a display of solidarity with the tea pickers and their environs.

The packets themselves were an innovation. The tea was brightly and individually packaged, and not sold loosely, that is scooped from a tea chest or tea drawer and funnelled into paper bags, as was the common practice. Customers didn't have to buy tea by the pound either. The tea packets were also available in quarter-pound and half-pound sizes. And he could, as he proudly boasted, sell a first-class tea at 1s 7d per pound as against the 2s 6d charged in other stores.

True enough, his competitors did not take this lying down. There were tea-tasting challenges, direct accusations of Lipton's chicanery articulated through handbills and critical letters and articles in the press – all of which Tommy absorbed and faced down.

And, well practised himself in the dark art of 'getting people talking', or 'spin', he made the most of his tea venture. He spun the myth, for example, that his innovative thinking had alleviated the physical burden of the Ceylonese plantation workers – their daily toil of carrying the heavy sacks of freshly picked tea leaves down the steep terraces had been substituted with a system of relay wires with hooks on which the sacks, once full and sealed, could be attached. In fact, other planters in Ceylon were already doing this.

Only two years had passed since Tommy had bought his plantations and he was employing 5,000 tea plantation workers and making provision for their families. Back in Glasgow he had created his own printing works, employing 180 people, and a packaging plant to compliment his tea warehouse of 400,000 square feet. He had even established a bakery in Glasgow. By the autumn of 1892, he was claiming that he handled more tea than any other firm in the world, turning over 150 tons per week – this rather inexact calculation being based on the expectation that each Lipton's Market would sell at least a ton a week.

As a further rebuff to his competitors he observed that up to twenty-five different teas were used in the blending of his teas. Who could compete with that or make such a rich blend? He gave further detail of how water samples were taken from the towns in which Lipton's Markets were to be situated to ensure the blend of tea was suited to the water of the district. Mindful as ever of his Irish and American constituencies, he was happy to state in interviews that the best water for making tea came from Ireland. However, again Tommy was not exceptional in this. In his native Glasgow, for example, tea merchants were blending and selling tea to grocers and each grocer had their own blend. As for the tea merchants themselves, their views of Lipton are generally not recorded, other than the reported pooh-poohing of his claims in the press from time to time. On balance, whilst Lipton's Tea undoubtedly hurt the business of tea wholesalers – since he effectively cut them out as middlemen – and British grocers in terms of tea sales, it is also true that Tommy's revolution in tea merchandising greatly stimulated overall demand and consumption.

Even in the 1920s, when his autobiographical *Leaves from the Lipton Logs* was written, he could not be modest in his achievement in the tea trade, and in fact it is a paradox in the life of Tommy Lipton that in one breath he could be so charming, genial, self-effacing and sportsmanlike when it came to playing the role of the gallant loser in the America's Cup and in the next reveal an embarrassing penchant for bragging and self-congratulation. The man who often privately referred to himself as the Great Lipton was not shy in celebrating his own achievements, especially when it came to tea. His timing and self-marketing had been masterful and he knew it. There is no doubt that his combination of marketing, personal reputation, networking, innovation and prudent planning all combined to create an association between his name and tea that continues nearly a hundred and thirty years later.

In spite of this astonishing rise from grocer to global entrepreneur in little more than twenty years, Tommy's own best years were still ahead of him. The years of Lipton as celebrity, Lipton as philanthropist, Lipton as creator of a world football tournament and Lipton as rescuer in the First World War were all still to come.

5

Reliance, the third challenge, 1903

In 1903, the year of Thomas Lipton's third challenge for the America's Cup, *The Wonderful Wizard of Oz* was the talk of New York. The show had opened at the Majestic Theater in Columbus Street in 21 January 1903, little more than ten years since Thomas Edison's electric lights had been strung along Broadway, giving it the new sobriquet of the Great White Way. *The Wizard of Oz's* grand total of 293 performances made it one of the longest-running shows of the decade, and its creator, Frank Baum, was living proof, if proof were needed, that it was possible to come to New York – the American epicentre of enterprise, power, wealth and multiculturalism – as a virtual unknown, and to succeed in a style and to an extent almost unimaginable anywhere else in the world at the beginning of the twentieth century.

Between 1865 and 1900 in particular the New York population exploded, rising to 3.5 million from less than 1 million at the dawn of the Civil War. Though not without its municipal and social problems, such as lack of sanitation and unemployment, New York was buzzing in the first decade of the new century, adjusting to the sounds of different languages and new customs. As honorary New Yorker and former editor of *The Sunday Times* and *The Times* Harold Evans has noted, 'New York had more Italians than Rome, more Jews than Warsaw, more Irish than Dublin and already more blacks than any city in the world.' In those turn-of-the-century years of peace, optimism and unfettered opportunity New York was a magical place, a kind of Emerald City.

Who knows the exact moment at which Tommy resolved to make his third challenge to the New York Yacht Club for the America's Cup, but it is hard to think of him watching his second *Shamrock* actually crossing the finishing line of the final race in 1901 challenge still unsure. Before long he was reminding friends that a shamrock had three leaves.

Was this third challenge a business decision? After all, Tommy was no Dunraven: he was not the personification of the elitist Royal Yacht Squadron nor, for that matter, the British landed classes, so the argument goes, but rather Tommy the grocer and tea merchant from Glasgow, or Ireland if you prefer, as the American press often did. He was Tommy the challenger, the self-made man, the supreme diplomat, the sportsman, the antithesis of the grand but distant wealth creators of America who defended the cup, the man of the people, and the real reason for his challenge, or rather the real victor, was Lipton's Tea. Its sales and reputation were enhanced by every utterance of its founder, who strode the world stage with a confidence that belied his humble origins. America's Cup racing was business, it is often argued, and Tommy had discovered to his delight that the inseparability of his name and his business was best sustained through repeated America's Cup challenges.

Yet this is too simplistic an explanation. Although Tommy was a simple man at heart, not vengeful or one to brood over disappointments, it is equally true to say that his choices and decisions were often made with a view to yielding more than one positive result. Of course Tommy knew that the publicity surrounding his third challenge would help to make him again the focus of attention, and he loved the status it gave him and the knowledge that that people were once more, on both sides of the Atlantic, talking about Tommy Lipton.

But third time around, business considerations were superseded by a deep-rooted passion for winning, which was always there before but was now inflamed by a second challenge that had come so close to victory. At the same time, Tommy felt he was within a boat's length of restoring British national pride. He would issue his third challenge, as he had done before, through the Royal Ulster Yacht Club, of which he was very proud, and hopefully bring the cup home to Britain early in the new king's reign, his friend Edward. The universal affection and gratitude that would have greeted Tommy on his return from the seemingly enchanted city of New York would also certainly have meant a great deal to him.

But, even more, Tommy knew that by winning the America's Cup he would be forever remembered. The paradox is that victory would have totally eclipsed any short-term business benefits that supposedly motivated the challenge. In short, it is absurd to suggest that Tommy saw this third challenge exclusively from a business perspective. It was a consideration but only that. By 1902 Tommy was completely under the spell of the America's Cup.

Year by year, since the announcement of his first challenge and the public listing of his company in 1898, Tommy had become more interested in activities that led him away, little by little, from the hands-on running of the business. Indeed, from the age of fifty onwards his passion for business was diluted by other passions that Tommy himself would not have regarded as distractions, but which nevertheless afforded him new, unanticipated pleasurable experiences. From 1898 Lipton's had ceased to be his sole *raison d'être*.

One such passion was cars. Tommy was said to have been the first person to own a motorcar in Britain – not even his friend the Prince of Wales beat him to it. And, with the national speed limit set at 12 miles an hour, Tommy achieved the distinction of being charged as a reckless driver, regularly exceeding this limit to the hazard of pedestrians and other road users alike. His first car was a 12-horsepower Daimler that he bought for £800 in July 1902. Yet Tommy's uniqueness of character was again on display when he managed to wreck this car within a matter of days while driving the almost traffic-free roads from his home at Osidge in Southgate to City Road.

Undeterred, Tommy was pictured only a few months later in October 1902 in front of his garage at Osidge with no fewer than six cars. The same month he was elected a member of the Royal Automobile Club. And yes, it had been observed by more than one policeman who had stopped Tommy on the road that if the third *Shamrock* sailed half as fast as Tommy drove his automobile to and from his office then the America's Cup was as good as won. However, the all-too-apparent aspect of his character that spurred on his indefatigable ambition to go faster, to win more, was tempered by other passions, which Tommy spoke of before embarking on the transatlantic voyage for his third America's Cup bid.

He was really a gardener at heart. At least that's what he told the women's magazines that interviewed him. Orchids were a particular delight, and could there be any better pleasure than an hour pottering about in the garden at the beginning of the day, and an hour at the end before darkness fell? Tommy thought not. He even presents to us an image of the flamboyant business tycoon becalmed, sitting alone with his thoughts, high up in the summer treehouse in his garden, the one with two specially constructed staircases leading up to it, undisturbed except for the rustling of leaves. At one with nature and contemplative, neither brooding nor melancholy, he absorbs the life-enhancing energy of nature. And after dark, when the tranquility of the garden could no longer soothe his spirit? He had no real appetite for reading or for the theatre. He was not a betting man and he could not be enticed to the card tables. When at home, his preference, it would seem, was to play billiards or to play the violin. Neither billiards nor playing the violin can be regarded as passions at any point in Tommy's life, however: they were merely pleasant diversions for a man whose life was predominantly business, and for whom the concept and reality of traditional family life meant nothing.

Throughout the rest of his life new passions would surface and evolve, but for now, in the autumn of 1902, his obsession with the America's Cup came to the fore once again. He wrote to the New York Yacht Club issuing his third challenge. For Tommy, this laying down of a third bid was straightforward and bold enough. It was a suitably gracious letter that requested no change in the racing conditions. The execution of this unprecedented third attempt to acquire the Auld Mug was another matter. Even though Tommy was now a hardened America's Cup campaigner and successful businessman of more than thirty years' standing, he faced a tough decision and one that would force him, and not for the first time in his history of America's Cup challenges, to fly in the face of one of his most cherished business principles: 'Never do business with an unsuccessful man.' There were only

99

two British yacht designers of the necessary stature and experience that were available to him. The first of these, William Fife, had failed with *Shamrock I* in 1899 and the second, George Watson, had failed with *Shamrock II* in 1901.

Which of these two could design a yacht sturdy enough to cross the Atlantic intact and yet swift enough to beat any sleek racing machine that Captain Nat Herreshoff could design? It was not an easy decision for a man who really had no practical experience of sailing and no real grasp of the technical precision required to produce a race-winning yacht. He knew enough, of course, to understand that length, sail area and displacement in the water were the key factors in determining speed and that because only the waterline length of the yacht and the sail area were regulated, yacht designers had their greatest scope for innovation with the shape and weight of the keel, the hidden under-water spine of the boat that runs from bow to stern. In spite of the defeats, Tommy was aware, too, of the deserved reputations of Fife and Watson on both sides of the Atlantic. Curiously, Watson's fame in yachting circles did not come from design after design of innovative racing yachts. Rather, he enjoyed recognition for the design of steam yachts like the 10-ton *Madge* and the much larger 90-ton *Vanduara*, which had made the yachting community sit up and take note of a young man who was daring in his designs, clever in his application of science and thorough in his testing. It had been on the strength of this combination and his closeness to Scottish thread manufacturer James Clark – who had commissioned the *Vanduara* and who was a prime mover in the 1887 Royal Clyde Yacht Club's America's Cup challenge – that Watson had been chosen to design the ultimately unsuccessful 1887 challenger, *Thistle*.

In light of this, it was all the more remarkable, then, that Tommy should have chosen Watson to design the 1901 challenger, because by that time Watson had failed three times, with the Earl of Dunraven's *Valkyrie II* and *Valkyrie III* following *Thistle*. In the small world of British yacht design, there was often no option but to do business with an unsuccessful man.

Unlike Watson, Fife came from an established family business of yachtbuilders, William Fife & Son. Both his grandfather and father were perfectionists and, over time, built up a reputation for delivering elegant, sleek race-winning yachts, among them the 40-foot cutter *Yama*, built for Mr Allen Ames of New York. Out of Fifes also came Class II yachts such as *La Poupée* and *Shulah*, with their 15-foot waterlines and overall lengths of 24 feet. There was, in addition, the 36-ton *Foxhound*, which won Her Majesty's Cup at Cowes in 1871.

The third William Fife, who acquired a similar celebrity as Watson as America's Cup challenger designer, was in a fortunate position when he came to play a full role in the family business in 1886, when he was twenty-nine years old and his father was sixty-five. He did not have the worry and uncertainty that his father and grandfather had suffered in previous years wondering where the next orders would come from: Fifes of Fairlie had been built into a solid business. However, in sharp contrast to his predecessors, William Fife III, known as 'The Boss', was not a man to share a joke or a beer with anyone in the yard, possibly because he carried the burden of not being the craftsman that his father, and grandfather, had been. He was no less passionate and obsessive about attention to detail, but he was a designer who drew up his plans and delegated. He also had no desire to share his work, or for that matter his life, with anyone other than was absolutely necessary. Even at the peak of public and media interest in the America's Cup Fife would give nothing away, making no statements and giving no interviews, not even in the build-up to the cup, nor in the aftermath. What's more, William Fife III kept no diary and left no correspondence other than that of a strictly business nature.

A very gifted yacht designer who, in the ten-year period before he was engaged by Lipton, had drawn up over two hundred yacht designs, a number of which became yachts for paying New York Yacht Club members, William Fife was taciturn to an almost painful extent. Boats were his passion, and when he wasn't working on them he had his mother and three sisters for company. He was also attentive to his civic and religious duties as a justice of the peace and an elder in the Church of Scotland. If Tommy Lipton couldn't possibly have been Scottish, as far as the American public and media were concerned, because of his charm, his storytelling and his style, then, in equal measure, the stereotypically strait-laced William Fife couldn't have been anything else. Still, everyone in the yachting community on both sides of the Atlantic knew of Fife's prodigious talent and his total commitment. It is not abundantly clear why George Watson sent Fife the detailed plans of *Shamrock II* a full eight months before Tommy delivered his third challenge. Nevertheless he did so, the only possible explanation being that he either instinctively knew, or Lipton had told him privately, that he would turn to Fife for attempt number three. Watson was hired as a consultant and back up to William Fife, whom Lipton appointed as the principal designer. The two men had been friendly rivals for many years. Out of their competition had grown a mutual respect. Once the challenge was official, Watson urged Fife to do testing at the Denny Tank in Dumbarton outside of Glasgow, as he had done with *Shamrock II*. At that time, the experimental tank at Denny's shipyard was unique, a resource that the Americans did not have. First commercially used in 1883, it was the creation of the insightful engineer

William Froude. Here, models based on a designer's drawings were constructed, shaped and tested in a tank 328 feet long, 23 feet wide and more than 8 feet deep with 365,000 gallons of water sloshing about in it. It was here that *Shamrock III* started to take shape. Models were built by pouring wax into a gap between a bed which formed the outer hull and a suspended linen and timber section forming an inner hull. The resulting rough model, or more specifically monohull, was first of all given a 'rough cut' by the model-shaping machine – then powered by steam. The machine, with its two cutters on either side, would cut away at the paraffin wax model, which passed up and down under the floor, pinned into a moving carriage. This went on until it was close to the designer's specification. The model, weighing approximately three quarters of a ton, was then lifted out of the carriage and, using planes, chisels and saws, the Denny workers would shape it exactly as the designer wanted it. Hoisted up, the model was then transported to the tank only feet away by a rail attached to the ceiling. The model was tested in the tank as if it was at its full displacement in the water, so measuring rods were used to weigh it down. It was then pulled up and down the tank in a carriage. In the tank a 4-inch wave was equivalent to a 6-foot wave in the sea. Today, the tank is now part of the Scottish Maritime Museum and is still used by students of naval architecture and engineering from Glasgow and Strathclyde universities. They use fibreglass models and can create 16-inch waves by pressing a button, but in 1903 wave generation was rather rudimentary, created as it was by the brawn of the Denny men. Still, the tank's rails were not flat, being cleverly designed to follow the curvature of the earth.

Yachts, cargo vessels, steamers and all types of ships commissioned from Denny's all began life in the tank. Denny's, as a shipyard, was by the turn of the century employing up to 1,500 people, approximately

15 per cent of Dumbarton's population at that time. The scale of the shipbuilding industry for this part of the Clyde alone is even more apparent when the Macmillans yard next to Denny's is also taken into account. Macmillans at its peak employed up to 600 people and built nearly 850 ships in total. Macmillans closed in 1932 whilst Denny's survived until the early 1960s.

Through the winter months of 1902 and early 1903 *Shamrock III*'s testing and then construction continued at a hurried pace. Her very existence was threatened at one point when a fire swept through Denny's yard. She survived but progress was slowed, and sadly the fire caused hundreds of redundancies. On 4 March Tommy visited the yard with his secretary and William Fife. By this time up to a hundred men were working on the yacht each day. Fife inspected every inch of the yacht.

There was a party atmosphere on the day of the launch – 17 March, St Patrick's Day. The workers in the Denny shipyard had been given the best part of the day off. By mid-morning hundreds of townspeople and visitors had moved towards the best vantage points they could find, either along the riverbank or on the water. The yacht builders R McAllister & Son came up with the novel idea of allowing the public into their yard for a better view, at a charge of sixpence per head, with the proceeds going to the Social Union Agencies.

The 3,000 bunches of shamrocks that Tommy had sent to Dumbarton for the Denny workers to wear on the day were distributed more widely so that many other spectators were also gaily decorated in green. *Shamrock III* herself was also adorned with a large shamrock for her big day.

The day's celebrations were set in motion when a train specially commissioned by Tommy left Glasgow Central station at 11.45. At just after 12.30 elegant ladies and top-hatted guests began stepping off the train straight into the shipyard. A select party assembled on the raised platform alongside the bow of *Shamrock III* at 1 o'clock, among them Lord Provost Primrose, Colonel William Denny MP, the Honourable Mrs Keppel, the Earl and Countess of Mar and Kellie, and the Earl and Countess of Shaftesbury. The latter, in her capacity as wife of the commodore of the Royal Ulster Yacht Club, had the responsibility of christening *Shamrock III*.

After 1 o'clock the band of the First Dumbarton Volunteers struck up with 'St Patrick's Day'. The guests were in position. The resplendent and very beautiful Countess of Mar and Kellie waved her black muff in the air. The men waved their hats and cheered as, echoing through the yard and up and down the Clyde, came the words, 'I christen you *Shamrock III*. May God bless you and may you bring back the Cup.' Smash!

As recorded on grainy black-and-white film, the sleek white *Shamrock III* glided effortlessly into the Clyde, her keel encased in a wooden container. The yard engines, fog signals and steam whistles of ships drowned out the shouts of 'Good Luck!' from all and sundry. The band played 'The Dear Little Shamrock' and shamrocks fell from the sky. All the while Mr George Wilson, member of the New York Yacht Club, looked on.

The lunch that followed for invited guests in the Model Hall at the yard was another mark of Tommy's generosity and extravagance. No less than thirty baskets of flowers, tied up with broad green ribbons and dripping with shamrocks, were suspended from the ceiling. The most striking feature of the tables was a symbolic display of intertwined shamrocks, thistles and roses. In the middle of the top table itself stood

a gold centrepiece filled with orchids, lillies of the valley, roses, shamrocks and thistles. Then the meal began: Potage Tortue Claire, Suprème
de Saumon à l'Imperiale, Galantine de Dine Trufée, Pâté de Veau,
Jambon de York, and Quartier d'Agneau à l'Anglaise, accompanied by
the finest of wines and followed by tea or coffee. There were speeches
of thanks and speeches of determination, then the special train was
ready to take the guests home.

The press reports in the following days on both sides of the Atlantic
echoed the optimism felt on St Patrick's Day on first proper sight of
Shamrock III. 'Bonniest challenger that ever kissed the Clyde',
announced the *New York Herald*. A broad consensus on this latest Fife
creation was reached by reporters, America's Cup observers and experienced yachtsmen alike: the new challenger was not only bonnie, she
had been designed for speed in New York conditions. She was a light-
weather boat, one capable of speed in the lightest of breezes and
equally well matched for a stiff wind. Her draught, or depth below the
waterline, was a little less than 20 feet. Her keel drew as much as the
defender she was to challenge but was shorter fore and aft, assisting her
manoeuvrability.

Her cast-lead keel was not a separate bulb but faired into the rest of
the boat. Its shape and weight had a significant bearing on the stability of the yacht and its speed through the water. She carried 95 tons of
lead, which in this instance was placed forward in bulk in a well-
rounded shape instead of being equally distributed. Her waterline
length was 90 feet, but her overall length was 138 feet. If two tennis
courts were laid end to end, *Shamrock III* would have stretched from the
baseline of the first court to more than half the length of the second –
past the net. Remarkable though it may seem today, *Shamrock III* was the
first America's Cup challenger to be steered with a wheel and not a tiller.

Even Fife and Watson declared, uncharacteristically, that *Shamrock III* was the finest specimen of the yachtbuilder's art that they had seen. Indeed, even those indifferent to yachting, or who had no appreciation of the yachtbuilder's skill, could see that *Shamrock III* was a beautiful yacht that was so obviously designed for speed. In short, *Shamrock III* was a bold design: a daring experiment, with a shape and style calculated to inspire confidence. Tommy was unquestionably pleased with the result and allowed all those invited to the launch to inspect her. This was a mistake as far as racing strategy was concerned and an unexpected gift for the Americans, who soon knew her every line and detail.

Between the euphoria of St Patrick's Day and the date of her departure for America in May, *Shamrock III* underwent numerous sea trials. At her helm was Captain Bob Wringe, widely regarded as the most capable yachtsman in Britain at that time and very knowledgeable of the American racing scene. He also had frontline experience of the America's Cup having served as first mate under Captain Hogarth on the first *Shamrock*.

With *Shamrock III* underway, being towed across the Atlantic on the least desirable voyage for any America's Cup racing yacht, attention focused on the defender. The revered designer Nathanael Herreshoff and the New York Syndicate now knew what to expect: a yacht that had won plaudits for her design, her speed and her innovation, the strongest challenger ever bound for New York.

When the White Star Line's *Oceanic* had arrived in New York in October 1902 she had been the bearer of a letter as eagerly anticipated as any of her first-class passengers. The New York Yacht Club's safe receipt of this letter, from Sir Thomas Lipton KCVO, representative of the challenge of the Royal Ulster Yacht Club, had set in motion the chain of events that now saw its author crossing the Atlantic some eight months later, on the same luxurious liner. The battle between *Shamrock III* and *Reliance* was less than two months away.

On this voyage Tommy had plenty of time to run over in his mind his tactics and decisions. Was there any more that he could have done, could still do to win the America's Cup? When he wasn't pondering the glowing press reports on *Shamrock III* or the spectacular launch celebrations, or even congratulating himself on the Fife–Watson collaboration, he had the company of other distinguished passengers to enjoy, passengers such as Charles Schwab, who had worked his way up from nothing to become president of the United States Steel Corporation, holding more than $10 million of stock. By the time Schwab was walking the decks of the *Oceanic* in June 1903 with Tommy Lipton he had only just turned forty but was one of the wealthiest and most powerful men in America.

Tommy was more than aware of the America's Cup media circus that would greet him when he docked in New York on 24 June 1903; his arrival alone would send America's Cup fever soaring up. In his transatlantic musings on America's Cup choices and decisions Tommy had reached the conclusion that time would tell who was the better designer, Herreshoff or Fife. In his heart, as his speech at a New York dinner hosted by President Roosevelt's adjutant, General Corbin, on the evening of the *Oceanic*'s arrival testifies, he really believed that this time Fife had the edge. If he was wrong, if *Reliance* did win, then it would simply be because she was the finest racing yacht ever built.

Such was the national respect for Sir Thomas Lipton, combined with the importance attached to the America's Cup, that Corbin had been dispatched by Theodore Roosevelt not merely to extend a greeting, nor even to host this reception and dinner at the Waldorf Astoria, but to invite him to lunch with the president at the White House. And within forty-eight hours of General Corbin proposing a toast to President Roosevelt as 'one beloved by all our people, respected by all the people of the earth' Tommy Lipton and William Fife were doing just that, one to the right and one to the left of 'the one beloved'.

This was the first of a number of meetings between Tommy and Teddy Roosevelt, one of the most able and dynamic of all American presidents, over the summer of 1903. The two men established a good rapport. Conversation over lunch was convivial – how could it not be with an animated raconteur and conversationalist such as Tommy? – and focused mainly on yachting and sport in general, although the president also diplomatically reiterated his policy of naval expansion. The generous hospitality, thoughtfulness and courtesy of the president was, however, most eloquently expressed in his presentation of ices in the shape of miniature yachts with the shamrock emblem and the stars and stripes intertwined.

How could anyone aware of this scene assert that this was only about selling more packets of tea from Tommy Lipton's point of view? How could anyone suggest that this was an American president simply currying favour with the British and the growing Irish-American community by recognizing the importance of a popular sporting event?

Though by no means a principal concern for Roosevelt, the America's Cup was nonetheless a useful promotional and diplomatic tool. On the one hand it fitted with his desire to impress upon Britain, and the increasingly nationalistic European nations, America's ascendancy on the seas. As a former assistant secretary of the Navy, Roosevelt – the man who had ordered Dewey and the Pacific Fleet to the Philippines to attack the Spanish Fleet of Admiral Montojo – believed in and cared deeply about maritime issues. His advocacy of a strong American Navy was a core element of his presidency. Even at the tender age of twenty-three he had written *The Naval War of 1812*, a book regarded as a classic and a copy of which was placed on every US ship thereafter. The America's Cup, and the public interest it aroused at home as well as in Britain and Europe, was an emotive manifestation of naval excellence, albeit in the spirit of sporting competition.

On the other hand, Lipton was no ordinary businessman of means. Roosevelt was fully aware of his diplomatic skills, which had come to light during his first challenge of 1899. Masquerading as an Irishman cloaked in 'shamrock' he distanced himself from Dunraven and the British aristocracy, yet he embodied the decency and gallant nature of the British people. Roosevelt knew, equally, that Lipton was a friend of King Edward VII and was also an extremely popular and famous celebrity in America. So much so, in fact, that when American tourists to Britain in 1903 were interviewed and asked who they would most like to meet on their visit, invariably the answer was King Edward VII and Sir Thomas Lipton.

During that summer of 1903, in the middle of the America's Cup hullabaloo, Tommy did indeed play a discrete diplomatic role with regard to two Irishmen languishing in British prisons. One, a former member of parliament, PA McHugh, had been jailed on charges of sedition, and the Irish-American lobby were campaigning for his release. The other, Colonel Arthur Lynch, was a journalist who had sided with the Boers and had been predictably branded a traitor. Tommy discussed the cases of both men with the president and passed on Roosevelt's views to the king when he returned later that summer. Edward intervened and by January 1904 both men were free.

Apart from time spent with the president, Tommy's diary that summer was packed with activity that had nothing to do with the America's Cup per se. His own progress was even somewhat presidential: he visited Chicago, he attended the Naval Review at Oyster Bay, he attended a beauty contest, he gave interviews and charmed everyone in his path. In true Lipton fashion he even found himself in the right place at the right time to save some lives. On 2 July, in New York Harbour, the bowsprit of the steam yacht *Allita* dismasted a much smaller vessel, the *Giralda*, during a sudden squall and caused her to capsize, catapulting her five occupants – two men and three women – into the turbulent waters. The *Erin*, Tommy's own luxury yacht, was moored nearby. He immediately ordered the lowering of two launches, jumped into one himself and led the rescue. The two ladies in question, Mrs Manderlick and Miss McClenahan, were more than happy to relate to the press their account of the heroic Sir Thomas. Tommy was made an honorary fire chief of New York and received a gold badge in recognition of his gallantry. For once Tommy could not have made it up. It was yet again publicity of the perfect kind.

Prior to *Shamrock III*'s voyage to America, she had also proved she could survive catastrophe. In a tragic accident during the eighth trial with *Shamrock I*, *Shamrock III*'s mast snapped and the steward, Paul Collier – who was also Captain Wringe's brother-in-law – was lost overboard and drowned. His body was not found for two weeks. Tommy paid for the funeral costs, including the transport to Collier's home of Wivenhoe, and he also ensured that his widow was not left in financial difficulty. The damage to the yacht and morale was, however, considerable.

Now, as she docked at Tompkinsville on the north shore of Staten Island in that early summer of 1903, *Shamrock III* had proved, as any

America's Cup challenger then had to, that she could endure an Atlantic crossing. This precondition of seaworthiness was regarded then, especially by the British not surprisingly, and is still considered now by yachting experts looking back, as an inherent and arguably insurmountable disadvantage. In comparison, the defender only had to outsail the opposition in racing trials in her own backyard. There are no modern equivalents in sport with such disparity, but it might be like asking a long-distance runner to compete with a sprinter, or requiring a Formula 1 car to drive hundreds of miles to compete on a racetrack on which its competitors have been testing their cars. Still, *Shamrock III*'s preparations were far better than those of her two predecessors: she raced in American regattas for weeks on end and had the added bonus of racing *Shamrock I* in the coastal waters off New York. Neither she, nor Captain Wringe, nor her crew, were by any means inexperienced or unprepared for the Sandy Hook racing conditions.

However, if *Shamrock III* was the finest example of the yachtbuilder's art, then the defender was truly the outstanding representative of the yachtbuilder's science. Only a month after there had been shamrocks galore on Clydeside thousands of spectators watched in awe as *Reliance* rolled out of her shed at the Herreshoffs' yard, Bristol, Rhode Island, to the strains of the 'Stars and Stripes'. Behind rails decorated with holly leaves and roses, her sixty-six crew members stood on her aluminium deck, proudly displaying the word 'Reliance' on their dark jumpers. It had taken four months and nineteen days to build this, the largest single-masted racing yacht of all time. In *Reliance* Herreshoff had taken the science of yacht designing to a new limit. It was as though he was deliberately poking fun at the America's Cup exception from the Seawanhaka Rule, a rule which heavily penalised racing yachts with extremely large sails and overhangs. Unlike the *Shamrocks*,

Herreshoff's defenders could dispense with concerns about seaworthiness.

Like *Columbia* before her, *Reliance* had a waterline length of 90 feet, but in her overall length she was 13 feet longer, measuring a breathtaking 144 feet. Her sail area measured 16,159 square feet, at least 2,000 square feet more than *Shamrock III*. Her rigging and sails rose to an unprecedented 175 feet. To keep her upright with such an immense spread of sails, her lead keel of 100 tons plunged 20 feet below the surface. *Reliance* was a yacht of extreme dimensions, the likes of which had never been seen before, nor have they been since. To put her in some context, the class of yachts, established in 1992, challenging for the thirty-second America's Cup in 2007 are built to a specified overall length of 79 feet with a draught of 13 feet. A typical main sail area is less than 2,400 square feet. *Reliance* had enough sails for at least five of today's America's Cup competitors.

But with size came the considerable challenges of steering, of weight and of storing and deploying so much canvas. Herreshoff installed nine winches below deck at the lowest and most central points of the boat to improve stability; this worked all the more effectively when the weight of the crew who had to operate them was added. The winches worked on ball bearings with automatically shifting gears, scientifically tested innovations that were simply light years ahead of what Messrs Fife and Watson were doing at the time. Whilst the British were pleased with their new steering wheel as a substitute for the tiller, Herreshoff achieved his own 'first' by giving *Reliance* two steering wheels and a hollow rudder which could be pumped full of water as needed for better control of the helm. He also employed light-weight steel spars so that the topmast could be retracted when the topsail was not set. Arguably, his greatest innovation was the placing of webbed steel frames that encased the hull and the deck. These were connected to the longitudinal frames that ran the length of the boat and to the bronze plating of the hull and greatly enhanced the strain capacity of the yacht. *Reliance* duly overcame the former defender *Columbia* and Herreshoff's other experimental creation, the flawed *Constitution*, in the trials to determine which of the three would earn the right to defend the America's Cup.

Herreshoff's steel webbing alone was truly radical and influenced boat and even aircraft design in years to come. Known as the Wizard of Bristol, he was at the peak of his powers and already celebrated as the designer of successful America's Cup defenders, but he was also an enigmatic and troubled figure.

Even as a boy Nathanael Greene Herreshoff was naturally serious, fascinated by mathematical data and energised by the application of trigonometry to boat design, his mind almost wholly absorbed by calculations of one kind or another. The playfulness of youth eluded him, and by the time he approached his teenage years in 1860 his world was dominated by family – he had no less than eight brothers and sisters – and the maritime environment of Bristol, Rhode Island, in which he lived.

His elder brother John Brown Herreshoff was blind, and it was Herreshoff's regular task to be the eyes and hands of this brother in their father Charles's large building shed on the waterfront. Together with their father they laboured for hours on end, measuring, shaping, carving, drilling and calculating the dimensions of the boats conceived and designed by both Charles and John. Some combination of his brother's quick temper, his own numerical dexterity and fear of disappointing his father reinforced in Herreshoff a desire for perfection in

1. Sir Thomas Lipton, the dashing grocer and entrepreneur. Unilever Archives

2. A typical Lipton's Market. Unilever Archives

3. A classic Lipton's advertisement with exotic images of Ceylon and a challenge to count the number of places the word 'Lipton' appears. The *Illustrated London News* Picture Library

4. On trial off the coast of New York, this angle of *Shamrock I* and *Shamrock III* shows off the awesome height and expanse of the sails. The *Illustrated London News* Picture Library

5. A major celebration at Denny's shipyard in Dumbarton as *Shamrock III* is launched in 1903. The *Illustrated London News* Picture Library

6. Sir Thomas at home at Osidge with his impressive collection of trophies. Unilever Archives

7. Sir Thomas at middle age, but still with an unmistakeable twinkle of youth and enthusiasm in his eye. The *Illustrated London News* Picture Library

8. The crew and *Shamrock IV*, the so-called 'ugly duckling' in racing action. The *Illustrated London News* Picture Library

Overleaf.
9. Sir Thomas at his best, entertaining guests at sea, including Rose and Joe Kennedy, second and third from the right. Unilever Archives

10. *Shamrock IV* measured against Nelson's Column in Trafalgar Square and compared with the defender, *Resolute*. The *Illustrated London News* Picture Library

11. A more thoughtful and pensive Sir Thomas having reached the age of 70, pictured in 1920. Unilever Archives

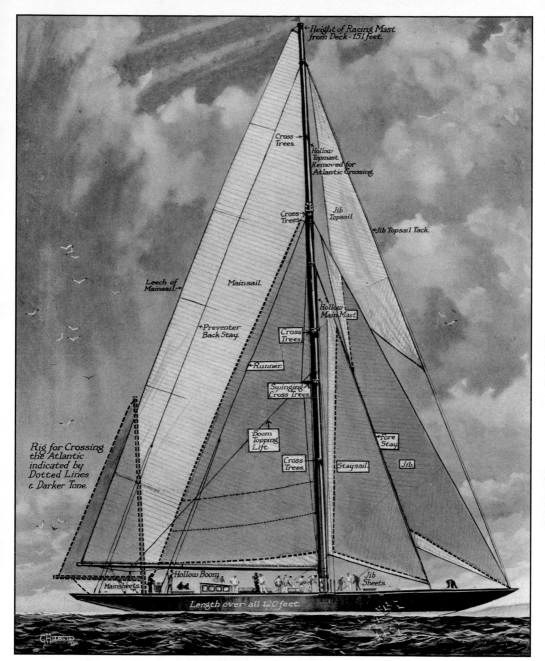

The labels within the image include:

Height of Racing Mast from Deck - 151 feet.
Cross Trees.
Hollow Topmast. Removed for Atlantic Crossing.
Jib Topsail.
Jib Topsail Tack.
Cross Trees.
Leech of Mainsail.
Mainsail.
Hollow Main Mast.
Preventer Back Stay.
Cross Trees.
Runner.
Swinging Cross Trees.
Fore Stay.
Boom Topping Lift.
Rig for Crossing the Atlantic indicated by Dotted Lines & Darker Tone.
Cross Trees.
Staysail.
Jib.
Hollow Boom.
Jib Sheets.
Mainsheets.
Length over all 120 feet.

12. A graphic of *Shamrock V* from the *Illustrated London News* of 1930 to show the contrast between the racing and transatlantic rig. The *Illustrated London News* Picture Library

Overleaf.
13. Great crowds gather on shore at Gosport to witness the launch of *Shamrock V*.
The *Illustrated London News* Picture Library

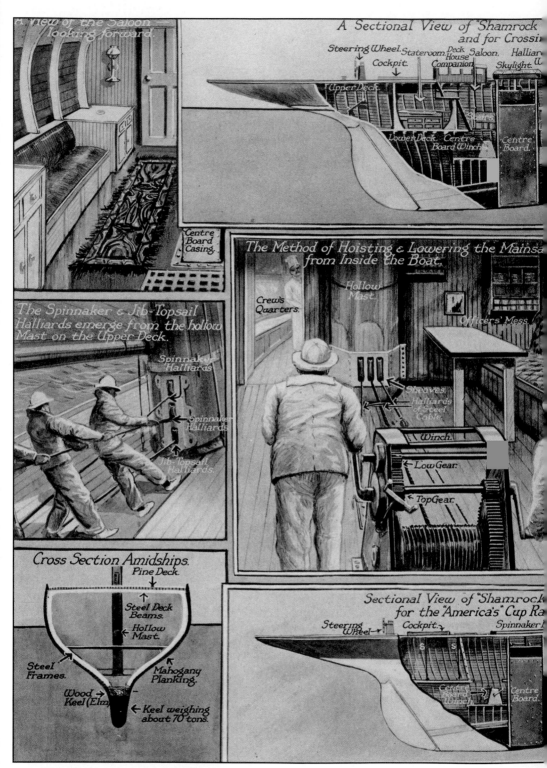

A View of the Saloon — looking forward.

A Sectional View of "Shamrock and for Crossi...

Steering Wheel. Cockpit. Stateroom. Deck House Companion. Saloon. Hallian... Skylight...

Upper Deck.

Lower Deck. Centre Board Winch. Centre Board. Stairs.

Centre Board Casing.

The Spinnaker & Jib-Topsail Halliards emerge from the hollow Mast on the Upper Deck.

Spinnaker Halliards

Spinnaker Halliards

Jib-Topsail Halliards.

The Method of Hoisting & Lowering the Mainsa... from Inside the Boat.

Crew's Quarters.

Hollow Mast.

Officers' Mess.

Sheaves

Halliards of Steel Cable.

Winch.

Low Gear.

Top Gear.

Cross Section Amidships.

Pine Deck.

Steel Deck Beams.

Hollow Mast.

Steel Frames.

Mahogany Planking.

Wood Keel (Elm)

Keel weighing about 70 tons.

Sectional View of "Shamrock for the "America's" Cup Ra...

Steering Wheel

Cockpit.

Spinnaker...

Centre Board Winch.

Centre Board.

14. A below-decks view of the technology and structure of *Shamrock V.*
The *Illustrated London News* Picture Library

...ed out for Racing in Home Waters
...Atlantic Ocean.

←Hollow Mast. Crew's
Spinnaker Boom. Hatch. Crew's Folding
Cots.

Crew's Quarters

Water Line.

A State Room –
looking aft.

...for Handling the Centre Board weighing nearly
Two Tons.

Centre
Board
Casing.

Sail Bin

...rds
...inch.

Man working
winch for
raising & lowering
centre board,
situated below
the lower deck.

← Cover.

How the Luff of the Mainsail fits
into a Slot in the Mast.

Mainsail.   Halliards.
                                   Track.
                          Block.

Luff Rope.

Mainsail→

Block.   Hollow
                                   Centre Mast.

Luff   Slide or Hank.
Rope
Fixing Eye.   Duralumin track running
down practically the whole length of the mast.

...ving how she will be stripped
Crew's Hatch.

←S=Stanchions.

Section of the Hollow Streamlined
Mast made of Spruce.

Mast & Topmast
built up in
66 sections.

Aft.   Fore.

Hollow
Centre
with
Sail
Halliards.

Mainsail
Track.

Walls 4 inches
thick tapering
to 2½ in. at top
of mast.

G H DAVIS
1930

Overleaf.

15. *Shamrock V,* pictured in May 1930, out in front, winning its first race in trials before the America's Cup.
The *Illustrated London News* Picture Library

16. The New York dinner of 1928 for pioneers of American industry. From left to right, Harvey Firestone, Julius Rosenwald, Thomas Edison, Sir Thomas Lipton, Charles Schwab, Henry Ford, Walter Chrysler and George Eastman. Unilever Archives

17. Sir Thomas is presented with a gold Loving Cup in 1930 paid for by donations of ordinary Americans, a remarkable gesture at the height of the Depression. The book beneath is filled with donor's tributes. Mayor Walker of New York holds the lid. Next to him is John Fitzgerald, former mayor of Boston and Sir Thomas's close friend. On the right is Barron Collier. Unilever Archives

this complex challenge. In fact, living in Bristol was itself a pressure in his young mind, for Bristol was about as centred on boatbuilding as a community can get. Between 1830 and 1856 no fewer than sixty boats had been constructed there, and it was home to men skilled in every conceivable discipline of boatbuilding, from carpenters to riggers. Added to this, several of Herreshoff's ancestors had been ship captains or ship owners, creating a family tradition that was difficult to live up to.

Having developed his analytical and sailing skills in this exacting environment, Herreshoff went on to study a course in mechanical engineering at the august Massachusetts Institute of Technology. Completing a three-year degree, he then accepted at the age of twenty an offer from the Corliss Steam Engine Company in Providence. Ten years later, in 1878, he went into partnership with his brother in the Herreshoff Manufacturing Company.

Herreshoff's output there verged on the miraculous, all the more so considering that he was neither physically or mentally robust, suffering from depression at various times in his life, and that his communication skills, never mind social ability, were absent most of the time. John F Kennedy may have been the most famous man ever to serve on a US Navy torpedo boat, but it was Herreshoff who made their development possible. When Herreshoff died in 1938, the files of the Herreshoff Company contained an estimated 18,000 drawings, the majority laid out or drawn in pencil by 'Captain Nat' as he came to be known.

Captain Nat designed winners year after year, and his yachts defended the America's Cup no less than six times. For this record alone, he deserves a place at the top table of designers in sport. But even before the first of these victories was recorded, his reputation went before him. When the 1893 challenger, Lord Dunraven, was asked whether his yacht, *Valkyrie II*, would win, he replied, 'I have a wholesome regard for the genius of Herreshoff.' Francis, Herreshoff's son, in his biography of his father, could not compile a list of all the races won by his father's yachts. Outside of the America's Cup two examples suffice: in the prestigious King's Cup, yachts designed by Captain Nat won in every year but one between 1912 and 1925, and in the most important annual race in the United States, the Astor Cup, his yachts in the schooner class won seventeen out of thirty-five races between 1890 and 1938. Such was the calibre of the designer of Tommy's opposition in 1903, but would the Wizard of Bristol's spell hold?

On the first day of racing, 20 August, *Reliance*'s captain, the by now familiar Charlie Barr, made the most of the upwind leg, outsailing the challenger but failing to beat the time limit. Though officially not defeated, the omens were bad for *Shamrock III*. The next race, on 22 August, started well enough. *Reliance* struggled in the oncoming swells and *Shamrock III* sailed ahead. Barr tacked, first to port then to starboard, turning *Reliance* for the wind to cross her bow, but *Shamrock III* had the advantage. *Reliance* was caught up in the drafts of wind from *Shamrock III*'s sails. Then, suddenly, the wind dropped and the sea lost its anger. Wee Charlie found smooth water; *Reliance*, no longer bouncing through the water dousing her vast sails in seawater, proved herself formidable. She reached the mark 3 minutes ahead and, with the help of her cutting-edge winch technology, lifted her vast sails with surprising speed. By contrast, Wringe's men on the *Shamrock III* semed to fumble with the downwind sails. *Reliance* sped off, her margin of victory a painful 9 minutes in the end.

Barr kept up the pressure at the beginning of the next race, but even so Wringe's crossing of the starting line a full half-mile behind *Reliance* seemed unforgivable. Still, to his credit, it was clear he was closing the gap. He switched to that giant headsail, the balloon jib, at the right time, but the ever-canny Charlie Barr then set his spinnaker, the huge three-sided sail forward of the mast, and *Reliance* catapulted forward once more. Wringe fought back, making a better job of the second turning mark than *Reliance*. As in the first race, the wind dropped again but *Reliance* was too close to home for it to matter. Wringe had to sail *Shamrock III* after her through the smooth windless water to the finish while the clock ticked off the seconds of his 3 minute 21-second handicap advantage. In the end, he stopped the clock 5 minutes after *Reliance*.

Delays followed as storms raged and races were postponed. At least *Shamrock III* actually crossed the starting line with *Reliance* the next time, but that was the closest she came to her in the whole race. *Reliance* even seemed to cope better with the choppy sea and she broke free of *Shamrock III*, leaving her in her wake. Both boats entered a bank of thick fog, but while *Shamrock III* lost her way, *Reliance*, with a pre-planned course to steer in the event of fog, sailed home to a jubilant crowd and the America's Cup.

President Roosevelt, special guest of honour at the Seawanhaka Yacht Club Dinner at Oyster Bay on 18 September 1903, stood up at the conclusion of the evening to offer a toast: 'I am now going to ask you to drink to the health of all of our gallant opponents of the last eighteen years, and especially the health of Sir Thomas Lipton whom we had hoped to have with us tonight.'

The president's toast was yet another salute for the man Americans loved to love. Tommy had lost again, but he wasn't loved as an easy opponent. On the contrary, he was loved because he was Sir Galahad: genial, amiable, suave, sportsmanlike, beaming, gallant, kind, generous – and a host of other adjectives employed by the American press. One *New York Times* columnist had even complained before the final dénouement of the 1903 America's Cup that in victory over Sir Thomas 'it would be utterly impossible to exult over him'. Remarkably, in the press reports that followed the races, Lipton's name was everywhere, but neither Captain Nat, nor Charlie Barr, nor the defender's powerful syndicate of JP Morgan, Vanderbilt et al rated much of a mention.

As the president spoke, however, Tommy was lying critically ill with gastritis in Chicago. Uncooked corncobs had been the culprits and Tommy was as sick as he had ever been. He was confined to bed for several days, and, without the timely intervention of a leading bowel expert, who administered a colonic enema, his condition could have been much worse. Tommy could do nothing but lie back and think about what might have been.

He had spent more than $2 million on his three challenges but hadn't won a single race; the Auld Mug was still in American hands.

Tommy's later reflections on his third challenge were still generous to all involved: 'Mr Fife produced in *Shamrock III* an exceedingly beautiful boat judged by the standards of these days. She was narrower and much longer than her predecessor. Once more we all thought that surely our time had come . . . While we had a good ship in *Shamrock III* the genius of Nat Herreshoff had built a bigger and better one in the *Reliance*.' He did allow himself, however, a dig at the extreme dimensions of the defender, for she was, in his view, 'certainly a freakish yacht in many ways and spread a tremendous amount of canvas, something like 16,000 feet, or fully 2,000 more than my ship'. But after this brief critical lapse Tommy recovered his usual tone: 'But that she could travel through the water she demonstrated conclusively by beating *Shamrock III* pointless.'

Even at the time, Tommy was generous in defeat and a paragon of diplomacy, and he could certainly reflect with some satisfaction on his achievements in the broader purposes of this third challenge, which, we have seen, were by no means just about selling tea. He cared too much about America and had become so obsessed with the fraternity and platform of the America's Cup, the enduring relevance that it gave to him, Tommy Lipton, as distinct from Lipton's, to be acting out of business interests alone. He had certainly played a very public and pivotal role in further strengthening Anglo–American relations yet again. Even in defeat he enjoyed the public attention, and when a lady tried to console him after *Shamrock III*'s defeat by suggesting quite seriously that the Americans had actually put something in the water, Tommy replied, 'I knew it all the time, madam. What they put in the water was the Cup's defender.'

6

Celebrity and philanthropy

Rose Fitzgerald Kennedy – the eventual mother of a president and matriarch of a dynasty – was in no doubt that any suggestion of a romantic liaison between her and Sir Thomas Lipton was absurd. The groundless rumour of an attachment had sprung from the occasion of a private dinner party in Boston when Tommy had proposed to Rose in mock seriousness. To the great amusement of all present she acted her role, turning him down and declaring him to be 'altogether too fickle'. Of course, he had been a visitor to her family home in Boston many times, and she had been a guest on board Sir Thomas's steam yacht, *Erin*, on several occasions, though always in the company of a host of others. That's because he was a great friend of her father, John Francis Fitzgerald, or Honey Fitz as he became known, a Democratic state senator and later mayor of Boston.

Honey Fitz was a great conversationalist, a man who prided himself on amassing knowledge and sharing it with others or using it as a powerful tool in political debate. Like Tommy, he was also obsessed with press coverage. At home he was always surrounded by newspapers, assiduously making press cuttings using his pen-knife and pinning them to his jacket. He was interested in every subject under the sun, especially politics and business, and in Tommy Lipton he found a well-travelled, well-connected business entrepreneur and celebrity whose particular blend of Irish–Scots badinage was a treat to savour. A further similarity was that Honey Fitz's father had also been a grocer. For his part, Tommy's intention in regaling his host with his tales was not the courtship of his daughter Rose or, for that matter, Agnes, with whom his name was also romantically linked. If anything, for the Fitzgerald girls and their little brother Thomas, this charming and loquacious associate of their father's cut an avuncular figure. As Rose later pointed out in her autobiography he was, in the kindest sense, old enough to be her grandfather, and she regarded him as a 'dear family friend'. Later, when her house in Beals Street, Boston, was converted into a museum, Rose ensured that a set of teacups and saucers, complete with their shamrock emblems, were on display.

From 1898 onwards, Tommy was undoubtedly a celebrity, both in Britain and the United States. The *Harmsworth Magazine*, London, for its April 1902 issue, produced small, square, nursery-styled ABC illustrations as a means of listing 'The Celebrities', placing one pre-eminent celebrity against each letter of the alphabet. E is for Edison, H is for Thomas Hardy, M is for Marconi, N is for Tsar Nicholas of Russia, V is for Jules Verne. Even Kaiser Wilhelm is there, as the world's number-one celebrity for the letter W, and amongst this illustrious company Tommy takes his place at L. In the United States, his America's Cup challenge in particular and the fact that his business interests brought him into contact with major operations in the food provisions industry, made it almost inevitable that he would be romantically linked with heiresses. One such was Alice Revell, who hailed from a wealthy family in Chicago, the city where Tommy had chosen to locate his meat packing business. An unforgettably named gossip columnist of the *New York Herald*, one Cholly Knickerbocker, even went so far as to claim that the 'couple' were about to announce their engagement at the end of August 1898. By this time Miss Revell was an established socialite and, if Miss Knickerbocker's reports were to be believed, ready to tie the knot – with an older man, true, but one that fell into the desirable category of wealthy, famous and popular. The story was, however, completely unfounded and an embarrassment to both Tommy and the Revell family. It was not to be the last. There was equally unfounded talk at one point of a romance with the daughter of Sir George Faudel Phillips, Lord Mayor of London.

Of course, such attention, for a man about to enter his sixth decade, was not entirely unwelcome. After all, Tommy courted the media like no other businessman, and cutting a dash as a sporting, wealthy Irish – as the American media almost always regarded him – charmer capable of sweeping a girl off her feet suited his purpose well. The point so often missed or downplayed about Tommy is his addiction to public affection, beyond all potential business gains: if he was not newsworthy, if he was not sought after, he was nothing. Fortunately for him, in the more socially restrained times of the late Victorian and Edwardian eras Tommy was the ideal celebrity on both sides of the Atlantic. As both media and socialites saw it, he was unencumbered with matrimonial or family baggage. He was neither pretentious nor pompous – at least not in public. He played himself up as the common man but never gave offence to the landed classes. He always had a tale to tell and was, quite simply, good company. As he moved through his

first three America's Cup campaigns he also built up a deserved reputation for lavish hospitality on board his own yacht.

For an American audience he was just the right blend of traditional
British gentlemanliness, gallantry, openness and humour. Invariably, he
presented himself with immaculate neatness and there was nothing
ostentatious about his dress: more often than not his coat and trousers
were a plain black-and-white striped wool; his white shirt was covered
by a buff linen waistcoat with pearl buttons – no gold, no silver, no
sparkling diamonds – and under his shirt collar he wore a black-and-
white striped silk neck scarf. He seemed to be both the embodiment
and the antithesis of Britishness at the same time, about as far removed
from perceived individual and colonial arrogance – as represented by
the Earl of Dunraven and the Boer War respectively – as it was possible to be, and yet as dignified, sporting and incorruptible as might be
expected of any 'Englishman'. In class-free America there was also an
admiration for Tommy's sheer entrepreneurial audacity, shaped and
sharpened as it was by early experiences in New York. He was, in his
own way, an American success story, loved all the more because he now
rubbed shoulders with presidents and royalty. Certainly the New York
Yacht Club, precious though it was about many things, did not share
the qualms the Royal Yacht Squadron seemed to have in offering Sir
Thomas Lipton membership.

Yet, in spite of all the hullabaloo surrounding Tommy's sensational
arrival on the America's Cup scene in 1899, and the remarkable graciousness with which he accepted defeat, his celebrity did not fully
begin there. In America, his profile went back as far as 1880. Having
looked at Chicago warehousing for his meat packing business, Tommy
had arrived in Washington, and, believing a particular day to be one of
the reputed open reception days at the White House, he enquired at

the front door of the White House if the president was at home and received an affirmative answer.

Rutherford Birchard Hayes, Harvard law graduate, three-term governor of Ohio and former Union general in the Civil War who had won the Republican nomination and then the presidency in 1877 amid accusations of blatant electoral rigging, was indeed at home. Mr Lipton was escorted to another room, where another man was waiting, a man whom Tommy took to be another secretary. They filled the time amicably enough with a lively and wide-ranging discussion, after which Tommy invited his new friend to join him for lunch after he had met the president. At this point his companion declared he was the president and had thought Lipton was another appointment he was expecting. It is likely that Tommy embellished this presidential tale ever so slightly but the timings do fit and the kernel of it is probably true.

In spite of this bizarre episode, and his advertising antics notwithstanding, Tommy's true celebrity status was attributable to two ladies, neither of them romantic attachments, who came into his life within a year of each other, in 1897 and 1898. Though neither initiated the contact, taken together they catapulted him into the top flight of world celebrities, bringing him to the attention of millions in Britain, Europe and North America and thus making him into one of the first major celebrities of the twentieth century. Their names were Alexandra and Erin, a princess and a steam yacht respectively.

Princess Alexandra, wife of Edward, Prince of Wales, was in her early fifties when she first encountered Thomas Lipton. She had come into this world in 1844 a royal princess of Denmark, born at the Yellow Palace in Copenhagen, the second of what was to become a total of six children for Prince Christian and Princess Louise. At eighteen years old, only four months after first setting foot in Britain, she married

Edward, in March 1863. Young, beautiful, elegant and fashionable, the princess was a warm and generous person who found it hard to turn down requests for help. She was also sensible, with maternal instincts and a desire to use her position as a force for good, and it is likely that Queen Victoria had sought the match with her son in the hope that Alexandra would restore in him a sense of duty and responsibility. Given that the arrival of this divine princess in Britain coincided with the development of photography and the advent of illustrated magazines, it is not surprising that this gentle, captivating Dane should have become one of the most talked about and admired people in the country.

More than thirty years on and six children later her husband was increasingly engaged, or sadly more often scandalously embroiled, in the high life, having been excluded from his mother's close circle of advisers. Alexandra had nonetheless lost none of her own desire to do some good, and in 1897, the year of Queen Victoria's Diamond Jubilee, she became concerned that thousands of London's poor, living in the overcrowded slums of the city, really had nothing to celebrate at all. In what appeared like a spur-of-the-moment decision she wrote a letter, to *The Times,* addressed to the lord mayor. She enclosed a £100 cheque for him and suggested that he organise a dinner for 'the poorest of the poor in the slums of London in the week of June 22nd at the peak of the celebrations'. It was a noble and well-intentioned gesture from a caring woman to whom acts of kindness came naturally. It was also, however, naive in the extreme. The letter was sent out in early May. On the day of its publication there was a loud thump in the lord mayor's office as the jaw of the incumbent – one Sir George Faudel Phillip – hit the floor.

The timing was terrible. Other Diamond Jubilee appeals were

already under way, including the lord mayor's own for the impover-ished and disabled children of London. Then there was the Indian famine. What the princess didn't realise was that for this dinner to be a proper dinner for all of London's poorest of the poor – an estimated 400,000 – £30,000 was needed. No flood of donations followed, and, as the lord mayor visibly aged, no one dared tackle the complex logis-tics without the money. All told, only £5,000 was in the kitty after a few weeks.

With less naive spontaneity than the princess, Tommy made a thinly veiled anonymous donation for £25,000, thus saving the day. The lord mayor now not only had his money, he had the support of a donor whose specialty was feeding people. Tommy revelled in the statistics of the operation: the feeding of the 400,000 meant that each would receive a 1-pound meat pie, a 2-pound loaf, 4 ounces of cheese and, of course, at least one cup of Lipton's Tea. Such a provision would weigh 700 tons, would fill about 400 vans and would take 16,000 men a full day to pack. Up to this point Tommy may well have been admired, revered even, as the Napoleon of the provisions trade, but as a personality in his own right he didn't really figure in the national consciousness. Certainly, no feature articles had been written about him in *The Times* before this date. Now, in 1897, through a single act of philanthropy, he became a nationally known figure, a celebrity. The princess was, of course, grateful too. On Christmas Day that year he received a diamond scarf pin from her. Speculation mounted and in the New Year's honours list of 1898 Mr Lipton duly became Sir Thomas Lipton, prompted, it was said, by the princess herself.

The interviews Tommy gave during this period were numerous and offer a good indication of the scale of his business at this point as well as more insight into his personal tastes. By his own estimation he had

1,800 staff based in his London works, including 500 women who weighed and filled paper packets with tea. At Cayton Street in London he also employed up to 800 in the manufacture of prepared cocoa, making chocolate and other confectionery. His impressive City Road headquarters in London, opened in 1896, were home to printers, architects, solicitors, marketing experts and accountants. The actual 'counting house' in the City Road building covered an extensive area of 6,000 square feet and was the workplace of some 300 clerks, book-keepers and female typists.

The principal feature of Tommy's own office in this hive of indus-try was the fireplace, adorned as it was with Indian patterns and elaborate carvings of oriental designs. Apart from this one arresting centrepiece his office was plain and wood-panelled, albeit with ten dif-ferent types of wood. An elegant portrait of Tommy seated at his desk in this same office was painted by the Dutch artist Professor Hubert Herkomer in 1896. Herkomer, who was also to paint a portrait of another of Scotland's famous sons, Lord Kelvin, was later knighted. Both paintings hang in the National Trust for Scotland's Hutchesons' Hall in the centre of Glasgow.

His mouth concealed and his jaw completely overshadowed by the spread of the handlebar moustache across his face, Tommy gazes out, relaxed and self-assured. There's no smirk or gloating in his eyes, but rather a look of quiet satisfaction. There is even a hint of melancholy. In moments of enforced stillness as he posed for the artist he would have been conscious of the gold frame on his desk beside him, the one that held portraits of his father and mother. It had been his special plea-sure to give them everything he could with his wealth – the comfortable house in the Glasgow suburb of Cambuslang, the horse and carriage for his mother, whatever money they needed – but he had been frustrated by their social inhibitions and lack of celebration for him. His father, Thomas, generous of spirit and nature, had been perennially cautious, completely lacking in ambition and guided by his station in life, passively accepting his lot. He had also been utterly devoted to Frances, and when she had finally succumbed to chronic bronchitis in 1889 he had rapidly declined, giving way to a broken heart and senile dementia. He had died a little more than a year later, in March 1890. Thomas and Frances were buried alongside John and Margaret, the two of their children who had survived their childhoods in Ireland and come to Scotland with their parents but had predeceased them some years earlier.

Six years later, there was still no wedding ring on Tommy's finger for Herkomer to paint. There is no hint from the portrait that he was anything other than a man of business, except the continuing importance of his parents to him, recorded in the presence of that gold frame. As he looked back on the 1890s nearly forty years later, shortly before his own death, he reflected on the loneliness that descended upon him in a world, as he put it, without any living relative. However, the man gazing out of Herkomer's painting betrays only the slightest hint of such sad reflections. Much more, the portrait shows a man who knows he has plentiful evidence of his achievements all around him, achievements obtained through his own initiative, drive and self-sufficiency.

Out of nothing – or, more specifically, out of a teenage decision that took him to America and gave him the skills and experiences that would change his worldview – he had created an empire. By 1896, the date of Herkomer's painting, he had passed the 300-stores mark. Reputedly, he had 5,000 agents worldwide, a packing house in Chicago where 2,000 to 3,000 pigs a day were 'processed' and a phenomenal 600 railway refrigerator trucks crisscrossing the United States, delivering meat to the US market. Around the British Isles he was employing at least 1,200 to 1,400 staff in his stores. To these stores, and through his worldwide network of agents, packets of Lipton Tea, with their distinctive yellow colour and Ceylonese branding, were distributed all over the world, printed in twenty different languages. And if he was conscious of the delicate golden frame next to him as Herkomer painted, then he could not have missed the giant frame on his office wall that held a cheque to Her Majesty's Customs, dated 30 April 1894, for £35,365 9s 2d, the largest amount yet paid for tea duty. As James Mackay noted in his biography of Lipton entitled *The Man Who Invented Himself*, by the mid 1890s Lipton was accounting for half of the total tea duty being paid weekly in the United Kingdom, and, as Tommy noted facetiously, he was probably paying for the government's intended naval building programme.

Yet along with new status and celebrity, Tommy's 'anonymous' act of spontaneous yet self-interested philanthropy towards London's poor in 1897 gave him something arguably more valuable: a realisation that the recognition and public affection he craved could come from sources other than his business success, extraordinary though that success was. Arguably, Tommy also recognised that the growth of the business was no longer entirely dependent upon his intuitive commercial acumen. Either way, the decisions he would take in the period of 1897 to 1898 would radically alter the direction of his life, ultimately defining who he was.

Tommy's own instinctive and irrepressible marketing prowess, built up over more than twenty-five years in business, had played no small part in changing high street retailing in Britain. He had contributed to and reinforced the trend in Britain for drinking tea rather than coffee. He had made that vital leap of expansion across the Atlantic, and he had a global network of agents and a vital string of supplier and retail business relationships in the lucrative North American market. Fifty years before branded products started to dominate the retail landscape, the image of Thomas Lipton was inextricably linked with both his products and his stores. And he had achieved all this without ever taking a loan or having a business partner.

Despite all this success, however, Tommy referred to his business as being in its infancy, and it is true that through its pattern of relationships, its strong retail presence, its international dimension and, not least, its reputation, it was poised for greater things. City analysts, however, took a somewhat jaded view of a business that they believed had reached a natural plateau, and with some justification: Tommy's formulaic grocery store business no longer had novelty value – it was taken for granted. His formula was also now more easily replicated or improved upon by smaller, more agile competitors.

This interest in the future of the business had arisen because of the abundant rumours and press speculation that Lipton was going to take the company public. Certainly, the working man and woman in the street, for whom Tommy Lipton had made life more bearable by making basic commodities more affordable, had faith in the man and his business. Without any diaries or personal correspondence it is impossible to know for sure what triggered Tommy's decision to float Lipton's. Perhaps he saw, before anyone else, that the business at its current growth rate was no longer sustainable as a one-man enterprise. Maybe he recognised that the additional perspectives and knowledge of a board of directors would generate more innovation and possibly strategic partnerships. Or maybe, deep down, Tommy just knew that he was now out of his depth and lacked the strategic brain to capitalise properly on the global opportunity that lay at his feet. Alternatively, his recently acquired national fame, thanks to his generosity for the sake of Princess Alexandra, may have set off a new train of thought in his mind.

Tommy was in fact nearly fifty years old. He had no living relative, no single person in his life that could replace the love and affection of his parents. He had poured his heart and soul into his own enterprise for more than a quarter-century. For all his bonhomie, banter and buffoonery, he could not have built a business on such a scale without shrewd decision-making, attention to detail, vision and, as Tommy himself repeated in streams of interviews, hard, hard work.

Already one takeover offer of £2.5 million had been made in that year of 1897, by Ernest Hooley, who had made his first million out of bicycles. Attractive though it might have seemed on the face of it, though it would have left Tommy with an unimaginable amount of money in the bank, it would also have left him with no business and, after the initial blast of publicity, no profile. Almost certainly, he never contemplated selling up and starting again – he was not a serial entrepreneur. Most likely, Tommy's calculation at this turning point in the summer of 1897, subconscious or not, was that the hard, hard work was behind him. In taking the company public there was an opportunity to spread the burden of responsibility and, at the same time, inject new capital and send out a very positive signal about Lipton's future prospects for expansion. These factors, combined with his own financial gain from the flotation, would allow more time and more wherewithal to devote to his new charitable persona.

By the summer of 1898 the die had been cast and the win–win scenario had not quite been realised. On the one hand, the public flotation of Lipton's had been an unqualified success, even though the prospectus had revealed the extent to which Tommy blatantly talked up his business. There were not 450-plus stores nationwide but 242. There were not 5,000 agents but fewer than 3,500. Even so, a capital of £1 million in cumulative preference shares; £1 million in ordinary shares of £1, for which a premium of 5 shillings was required on each share purchased; and £500,000 of debenture stock to be redeemed after September 1920 at 115 per cent was offered. The public response was truly astonishing: police were required to manage the crowds at the Glasgow branch of the National Bank of Scotland, and literally tens of thousands of applications arrived by post. The business press reported that only the flotations of Guinness and Allsopps were even comparable, but that the queues and the demand for 'Lipton Limited' were unprecedented. As widely reported, Tommy himself made £2,466,666 from the sale. He retained a majority shareholding, and it appeared that Tommy, his trustees, his financial adviser Panmure Gordon, the City and, not least, the share-buying public were all satisfied with the outcome.

On the other hand, Tommy betrayed his unease with his new status as accountable chairman and chief executive at the first shareholders' meeting on 2 June 1898, at the Cannon Street Hotel in London. He gave a faltering address and failed to exude his usual charm and self-confidence. He was challenged on his announcement of seeking to take Lipton's into beer, wine and spirits. For Tommy, who normally possessed such an impeccable sense of timing, such an announcement was itself bad judgement. If ever there was a time for Tommy to demonstrate how the new company could provide both stability and growth by 'sticking to the knitting' this was it. However well the flotation had gone, Tommy had lost his bearings and his composure.

Nevertheless, in this flotation, despite his new accountability, a

133

switch seems to have flicked in Tommy's brain. Hard work was still ahead of him, he could see that, and he could not divorce himself from the business to which he had given his life, but the days of hard, hard work were now behind him. He would no longer live and breathe Lipton's. He didn't need to. More importantly, he didn't want to.

Inspired by the success and opportunity of the Jubilee Dinner he thought up the idea of investing £100,000 in a chain of twenty-five restaurants for the poor, charging the lowest possible prices for fare that was basic but filling. It was classic Tommy thinking, combining doing the right thing for the people most in need with a business proposition that cut out the middleman and would have great potential for publicity. The ultimate prize would be people everywhere talking in glowing terms about Tommy Lipton. However, the idea bombed, as restaurateurs and tea and coffee house owners made loud protests. Fearful of the impact on his core business, Tommy withdrew.

His involvement on the committee of the Alexandra Trust also left him exasperated. The trust's goal was to provide meals to poor children at little or no cost, mainly in London. The trustees included the princess herself, the Duke of Norfolk and Sir Francis Knollys, who was a member of the royal household, but not Tommy. Though the trust was successful in its own way, setting up 200 food centres in London, it seems such a waste not to have given Tommy a more prominent role. Given that he had the best credentials of all, with his philanthropy and business knowledge, it seems a deliberate snub, the result of ingrained prejudice perhaps, and one that appears all the more bizarre in hindsight given the honour that had been bestowed on him and the bond that Tommy was to nurture with Princess Alexandra's husband. Considering the fact that Tommy was to become, in the space of a few short years, one of the most talked about people in the world and that the Alexandra Trust itself continued up to the Second World War, it is remarkable that he was not drawn in further to this cause and the inner circle of its trustees. If asked, he could not have refused. From his perspective, he had experienced, as he had done with the flotation, an initial elation, seeing a new multidimensional opportunity open up in front of him, only to discover that, for the first time since his formative experiences in America, others were telling him what to do. He had to play a leading role, but he was not given free rein to take centre stage.

Even though he had bounced back from his first encounter with shareholders by securing a major new contract with the army, the summer of 1898 was not filled with the contentment that it should have been. Both the flotation and the Jubilee Dinner donation could have been springboards to a more lasting legacy, and he had in fact made numerous individual acts of generosity, usually in response to appeals made straight to his face. He had also, for example, shown great compassion for striking textile workers and for his own employees who found themselves in difficult situations. However, after his fingers were burnt by the failed restaurants idea and his marginal role in the Alexandra Trust, he made no further attempts at linking his business with his own philanthropy and his good name.

He did not stop giving – he contributed to a number of public appeals, especially those endorsed by Edward – but he was by no means in the top flight of philanthropists of his day. This became particularly apparent when speculation in the press mounted with regard to the identity of the major donor of £200,000 in support of King Edward's quest to build and maintain a new sanatorium for sufferers of tuberculosis. Tommy's friend Andrew Carnegie, who by that time had given away an estimated £15 million, was a possibility, as was Lord Iveagh,

135

who was known to have given a sum of £250,000 to the Jenner Institute of Preventive Medicine for research in bacteriology. The latter had also given a similar sum for workmen's housing in Dublin. In addition, the Duke of Devonshire, Cecil Rhodes and even Pierpont Morgan, the American banking magnate and America's Cup defender with whom Tommy was by now well acquainted, were all considered capable of such largesse. Tommy, who collected these press cuttings where they mentioned his name, was featured only at the bottom of this list. He would also have been aware of the other notable businessmen within living memory who had set new standards in philanthropy. One of these, another retailer, by the name of David Lewis, had given £1 million for hospitals and recreational buildings for the people of Liverpool and Manchester. Birmingham had cause to be grateful to Sir Josiah Mason, who had expended £430,000 on orphanages in the city. Another, Thomas Holloway, who made his fortune from ointments and pills, had immortalised his name by giving £700,000 to Holloway College. Arguably, however, the philanthropist who should have caught Tommy's attention more than any other was George Peabody, the man of whom Gladstone, the British prime minister, said, 'he taught men how to use money and how not to be its slave'.

George Peabody should have been an important name in Tommy's reckoning for four reasons. Firstly, it was Peabody's financial empire that became the House of Morgan and was now presided over by Pierpont Morgan. Secondly, undoubtedly Peabody did have a genuine and sustained desire to help London's poor, the beneficiaries of Tommy's largest philanthropic gesture to date. Peabody donated £500,000 to them, particularly for housing. Thirdly, the sheer scale and depth of Peabody's concern for humanity set him apart from other generous givers in the business world. Having amassed a personal fortune of some £20 million as a banker and financier of the merchant trade in the 1850s, George Peabody's own road-to-Damascus conversion to charity occurred at the end of the American Civil War. Though a Unionist he established a Southern Education Fund to provide new and equal educational opportunities for both white and black in the defeated and demoralised south. It was the first of many outstandingly innovative philanthropic acts that encompassed issues as diverse as natural history, palaeontology and, of course, London's poor.

Finally, George Peabody established the Peabody Trust in 1862, ensuring that his name would be known to posterity. The trust continues to this day, managing nearly 20,000 properties across London which house up to 50,000 people. Not only that, educational and scientific organisations across America bear his name. Peabody carried no ideological baggage and did not link his philanthropy to religious zeal. He became quite simply a paragon of American virtue who built more bridges between Britain and America through his charity than any politician could do at the time. He was the first American to be given the Freedom of London.

In fact, the gift of £200,000 for the sanatorium had been made by Sir Ernest Cassel. Cassel, the youngest son of a banker from Cologne, had become a prodigy of international finance, building his own wealth through interests as diverse as American railways, Swedish iron ore and South African diamonds and gold. He was the king's own financial adviser and enjoyed the reputation of having helped Edward ascend the throne debt-free. Yet, in spite of his royal connections and even though he had converted to Catholicism following the death of his wife of tuberculosis in 1881, this private and unassuming man was labelled pejoratively by some in the upper echelons of British society as a self-made German Jew. Surely only those of the appropriate lineage and inherited associations, they said, should be counted among the confidants and companions of the royal family. In that sense Cassel and Lipton were two of a kind, feted by kings, prime ministers and politicians, but frowned upon by an element within the divinely ordained aristocracy.

Also like Tommy, Sir Ernest Cassel left no diaries or correspondence. The difference is that he is remembered today for his philanthropy. In his lifetime he made donations in excess of £2 million, principally for science, medical care and research and the establishment of the British–German Foundation. It is a tragic irony that the tuberculosis that robbed him of his wife and prompted his £200,000 gift was also to claim his daughter's life nine years later.

Whilst the names of Carnegie, Cassel, Peabody and the others continue to evoke gratitude, the name of Lipton usually only produces the response 'as in tea?' Nearly eighty years after his death there are no buildings, colleges or foundations in his name. In his native Scotland he is not celebrated or remembered in any particular forum or environment. He is not acknowledged or regarded as one of the great sons of Scotland.

From a cynic's perspective Princess Alexandra unwittingly gave Tommy Lipton a celebrity status he did not deserve. He proved himself, they would argue, merely a token philanthropist who was not even in the same league as his friend Carnegie. He had the money, he had the opportunity and through the Peabodys and the Cassels he had the inspiration. His relative insignificance in terms of philanthropy – comparisons with the Rockefellers and Vanderbilts, other combatants of the America's Cup, don't bear thinking about – are ample proof, his past and more recent detractors have said, of a man who simply used philanthropy, and, for that matter, celebrity, as it suited him to satisfy his voracious appetite for publicity and sales.

All too often Tommy Lipton has been regarded as a one-dimensional self-seeking publicist, a man who rejoiced in his daily shave for the time it afforded him to gaze upon himself. Just as his America's Cup challenges have been judged mere exercises in self- and business promotion, so have his philanthropic acts. Tommy Lipton has not been accorded substantive references in any biographies of Queen Alexandra to date, in spite of what he did to spare her embarrassment in her mother-in-law's Jubilee year of 1897. Nor does he merit more than a few lines in more modern era-driven histories of the Victorians and the Edwardians. Such brief mentions as there are reduce Tommy to a crony of Edward VII or trot out Kaiser Wilhelm's oft-quoted remark that King Edward was unavailable because he was out yachting with his grocer.

In truth, his philanthropy was spontaneous and reactive for much of his life. He gave generously to those in need who crossed his direct path, but he had little time for more complex, or arguably bureaucratic, mechanisms for the delivery of relief to the poor. After his initial involvement with the charitable work of Princess Alexandra, he decided to be more true to himself and not to get involved in organised philanthropic activity. His belief in taking direct action was to become much more apparent later in his life.

Along with charitable giving, Tommy also seems to have been written out of other areas of interest. He is nowhere to be found in *100 Years of Football: The FIFA Centennial Book* or other accounts of the history of the beautiful game, despite being the instigator of international football tournaments in Europe and Argentina. Uruguay and Argentina competed for a Lipton trophy, which Uruguay won – their first international success, twenty years before they became the first winners of the World Cup. And in 1910, long before the official European cup competitions were established, the likes of Juventus, Stuttgart, Red Star of Switzerland and a successful but lowly team by the name of Woolwich Arsenal from England's County Durham were competing for the Lipton Cup in Turin.

It is certainly true that Tommy could not change the colour of his spots to embrace, for example, a more structured longer-term approach to giving. He was energised by his own spontaneity and his reliance on a deep-rooted belief that he, Tommy Lipton, could see it through on his own, whatever 'it' was. As Lipton's 1950s biographer Alec Waugh put it little more than twenty years after his death, Lipton was 'one of those who have to do everything in just the way they want'. In this sense he certainly possessed an arrogance, and one which has worked against his memory. Between close friends and behind closed doors he referred to himself as 'The Great Lipton'. He could not cope with the consultative and collaborative nature of charity work, especially in the case of the Alexandra Trust where he had to listen to people who knew much less about the supply of provisions than he did.

For examples of the more enduring reputation and legacy that Tommy might have had one need only look to two other Glaswegians who were, like Tommy, hard men of commerce, men of retail. Sir Isaac Wolfson (1897–1991), like Tommy, was born into a family on the lower rung of Glasgow society. His father and mother, Jewish immigrants from Russian Poland, taught Isaac and their other eight children the virtues of hard work and self-sufficiency. From making frames in his father's workshop, Isaac went on to become a salesman, selling clocks, mirrors and eventually clothes. After joining a Manchester-based mail-order company, Universal Stores, he helped to transform it into one of Britain's most successful retail conglomerates in a career lasting forty years. In the 1950s an estimated quarter of Britain's population were its customers.

When Sir Isaac died in 1991 Great Universal Stores was making annual profits of £400 million. Sir Isaac himself had had no doubts about what his own wealth was for. In 1955 he set up the Wolfson Foundation, believing, in accordance with his own family and religious traditions, that the redistribution of acquired wealth for the public good was a moral responsibility. Colleges in both Oxford and Cambridge now bear his name. In Glasgow, where he was given the Freedom of the City in 1971 – Lipton had also been given this honour in 1923 – his foundation is visible in hospitals, medical schools and universities. Overall, the Wolfson Foundation awarded grants of more than £30 million in its first twenty years of existence. It continues to be an active and major grant giver in Britain today, and the legacy of Sir Isaac Wolfson will endure for a long time yet.

The other outstanding Glaswegian philanthropist is Sir Hugh Fraser (1936–87). When he was just twenty-nine years old Sir Hugh inherited his father's millions and his department-store business, of which he had already been a director since he was twenty-one. Sir Hugh made a success of the business and, shortly after his father died, profits in House of Fraser rose from £5 million to £35 million. The company would ultimately grow to be worth £750 million in his tenure, but his own life became clouded by the complexity of two failed marriages, some major business setbacks and a weakness for gambling.

What's strikingly similar about Sir Hugh and Tommy is that they were greatly influenced and inspired by their mothers, and it was in his mother's memory that the former created the Hugh Fraser Foundation with capital of over £2 million. The first contrasting point is that Tommy had no direct example of philanthropy to follow in his parents, while Sir Hugh did. His father was very generous with his money, particularly for hospitals and research institutes. After his death the

Fraser trustees bought the sacred island of Iona for the Scottish nation. Still, he shared Tommy's addiction to publicity and, like Tommy, he also connected with ordinary people in spite of his wealth and fast living. He took regular, almost daily, counsel from his mother. Most notably, and in sharp contrast to Tommy, he retained his headquarters in Glasgow, in Buchanan Street to be precise. He never lost his Glasgow accent or his close affinity with the city.

Admittedly, it is easier to recall a man when the stores carrying his name still stand, and House of Fraser continues to trade while there are no more Lipton's Markets on the high street. Even so, the legacy and memory of Hugh Fraser will still be more enduring than Tommy Lipton's thanks to his philanthropy and foresight in establishing a foundation, the terms of which he allowed the trustees to change, though retaining the broad remit of supporting causes in the West of Scotland. For Sir Hugh realised that society's needs change and that particular needs can be met entirely. He did not want his foundation to become obsolete because its charitable purpose was no longer valid.

Tommy did not lack the generous nature of either Sir Isaac Wolfson or Sir Hugh Fraser. He loved his native city too and he was to remark jokingly later in life that 'only the duffers leave Glasgow'. Given what he achieved in his life, in business and on the world stage, it is a pity that he neither sought nor created an enduring mechanism that would have reminded his Glaswegians, his fellow Scots, Britain and indeed the United States of a dynamic and generous life.

Instead, Tommy responded to what was put in front of him. He was not bitten, as Sir Ernest Cassel was, by the brutal experience of tuberculosis. He did not have the example of working and giving inspired by faith Isaac Wolfson later had. He could not look up to his father's shining example of charitable giving as Hugh Fraser was to do. Tommy was prompted instead by his own first-hand experiences of poverty and hardship. Ultimately, his philanthropy, as we shall see, was shaped by a myriad of unremarkable kindnesses to people whose needs were presented to him directly. Princess Alexandra opened the door to a more structured and prominent philanthropy, but because he couldn't do things his way he walked away. Still, he had ahead of him one more major act of philanthropy.

Despite considering a cup challenge in 1890, Tommy asserts in his memoir *Leaves from the Lipton Logs* that it was 1898 when his thoughts turned again to his boyhood passion – not sailing, for he never was and never would be a yachtsman, but the sea. He sought 'more frequent respites from the cares of business'. As always with Tommy, it not quite clear what came first, the idea or the opportunity, but he learned that a large steam yacht, christened *Aegusa* as recently as 1896, originally commissioned for Signor Ignatio Florio of Palermo and built by Scott's of Greenock in Scotland, was available for purchase.

The *Aegusa* was impressive. One of the largest yachts of her time, she had a waterline length of 252 feet, an overall length of 287 feet and a beam of nearly 32 feet. She was powered by a four-cylinder triple-expansion steam engine working single screw, which contributed to giving her, from her two boilers, a speed of 15.6 knots. She was designed for opulence and Tommy, when he acquired her for £60,000, did not betray the intention of the original commission.

Remaining true to his Irish heritage and mindful of how well the ambiguity of his Irish-Scottishness played, he decided to rename the vessel *Erin*. Her distinctive yellow funnel towered above a teak deck-house and a large open area of polished deck, covered by awnings as the occasion and sea conditions merited. Two smaller masts allowed for the frequent raising of bunting and at times for the raising of sails in rough weather.

Quite apart from her construction she was unlike other luxury yachts of the time for the simple reason that her owner combined warmth of welcome and generosity for all her guests with a degree of style and comfort that was less in evidence elsewhere. Below decks, *Erin*'s bedrooms, with their large gilt beds, were laid out in laces and silks. Clocks, gleaming brass, bronze statues and ornaments, royal blue Sèvres vases, china cabinets and watercolours by the Chevalier de Martino and Parker Newton that hung from the bulkheads impressed even the most travelled of the rich and famous that were invited on board. *Erin* could also boast a dining room that ran virtually the length of the ship, and on the starboard deck luncheon tables could be set up to serve seventy at a time. A harp stood proudly in the music room, where canaries were also in residence. And as the sun set, the *Erin* was illuminated above and below decks, including her masts and rails, by 3,000 iris blue lamps.

But all of this would have counted for so little had Tommy not been such a gracious and witty host. How hard it must have been on those multiple America's Cup race days to smile and entertain through defeat. On non-race days, as described by the New York journalist Dorothy Dix, entertaining was on a set pattern. Afternoon tea would be served at three. This would normally comprise hot crumpets, tea presented on individual trays with the saucers on top of the cups, a slice of lemon, two lumps of sugar and a miniature milk jug shaped like a dragon's head, broiled birds and champagne. This may seem an extraordinary combination for more modern tastes, but it was one that was entirely in keeping with Edwardian gastronomic delights. A formal dinner would be served at nine each evening.

Pierpont Morgan famously used his *Corsair* steam yachts as neutral and safe territory for business negotiations. It was on *Corsair*, for example, that he settled the dispute between the New York Central and Pennsylvania railroads. The tobacco tycoon Jacob Lorillard made such a point by purchasing a new yacht every year, whilst the Philadelphia banking millionaire Anthony J Drexel made it his special boast that few in the world could afford the crew of ninety-three or the maintenance for his modest 323-foot steamer *Margarita*. Still, even Lorillard and Drexel's boasts of yachting luxury are paltry in comparison with what William Kissam Vanderbilt could have said about the truly majestic *Alva*. Named for his wife, she cost $0.5 million to manufacture in 1886 and around $5,000 a month to operate. When she was launched, 10,000 people lined the shore of Wilmington, Delaware, to witness the birth of this awesome symbol of opulence. Her elegant exterior was more than complimented by an interior that included state rooms, each panelled in different wood; a dining salon of white enamel, ornamented in gold, and a library of French walnut wood panels, 18 feet long and 16 feet wide.

Tommy was not thus inclined, nor was he wont to make comments about his yacht reflecting his importance as others did. Rather, it was the combination of the quality of his entertaining, his amazing sportsmanship in defeat and also his outstanding courtesy and hospitality for all of his guests that truly enhanced Tommy's reputation and celebrity. For Tommy, *Erin* became a second home, quite literally a vehicle to expand his horizons. On *Erin* he could also do everything his way: he was the captain; everyone on board was his guest, his responsibility. And, as her visitor book and photographs show, Tommy was sailing with living history, playing host to the likes of Thomas Edison as well as guests from other yacht clubs all over the world. Imagine the diplomatic and conversational skills required for lunch with King Edward VII or President Roosevelt or possibly King Constantine of Greece, King Alfonso of Spain even, or, arguably the most daunting of all, Her Majesty Empress Eugenie of France. The most historically significant figure in political terms to board the *Erin* was Tsar Nicholas II of Russia.

Who could have believed that between 1898 and the outbreak of the First World War in 1914 the name of Tommy Lipton, through the America's Cup and *Erin*, would be known and recalled with affection by the monarchs and leading figures of the day? And his hospitality on *Erin* was reciprocated on the Riviera, in Greece, in Spain, at Cowes, Sandringham, Balmoral, Ascot and, of course, across the United States, where he was feted almost like a visiting ambassador. These were golden years for Tommy. He interspersed hard work with a social calendar on the ocean waves that was second to none.

Sadly for Tommy and the world these years were coming to an end, as the dark clouds of war gathered on the horizon. When war did break out in 1914, Tommy, a man in his mid sixties, had every right, given the nature of his business, to expect a call from the War Office requesting assistance and offering some London-based co-ordinating role in supplies. It didn't happen that way at all. Tommy's war effort was instead prompted by the Duchess of Westminster, who suggested that his yacht be converted into a hospital ship. Tommy had lost none of his spontaneity and rose to the challenge, quickly converting *Erin*. He equipped her with medical supplies and equipment, ten doctors, twenty nursing sisters and more than sixty orderlies, then dispatched her across the Channel. But Lord Kitchener was not impressed. Both Tommy and the Duchess of Westminster were criticised in the press for this so-called amateurish gesture. Even so, *Erin*, who now reverted to her original name of *Aegusa*, was required for service in the Mediterranean, where she was required to transport medical supplies between Marseilles and Salonica. Tommy went with her when he could so easily have stayed at home. Not only that, he met the entire cost of the expedition, just as he had the refitting of the ship and the first cross-Channel trip to France.

From Salonica he travelled more than once by train to Serbia. Here he witnessed, by his own account, 'the unspeakable agonies of the typhus epidemic which did such havoc among the Allied troops in that country'. At one point whilst in Belgrade he was subject to an Austrian bombardment, but he was not so close as to be in mortal danger. Nevertheless, he was there, in besieged Serbia and putting his life at risk, all the while funding his own humanitarian war effort. And even in war-torn Serbia his admiration for American people was enhanced, for he encountered a selfless man, Dr James Donnelly, who had sacrificed his far less traumatic post as medical officer for the Port of New York for the treatment of countless typhus patients. It greatly grieved Lipton later to learn that Dr Donnelly had been overcome by the disease.

Tommy made a second trip to Serbia and Montenegro and further trips to Salonica, where he also delivered medical supplies. In between, he authored articles at home that drew attention to Serbia's plight, the courage of the soldiers and, of course, the bravery of medical men like James Donnelly.

By 1916 he had to hand over *Erin* to the Admiralty for patrol work. In good times and bad Tommy had built up a remarkably strong bond with the crew who sailed her. Even when not on board he tried to keep in touch with them, especially in this time of war. Now equipped with guns, *Erin* succeeded in her new duties, sinking an enemy submarine in April. But her luck was to run out in a matter of days when she hit a mine and sank in the Mediterranean. Tommy was heartbroken. 'My beautiful and historic yacht went to the bottom of the sea, carrying with her, alas! six members of my crew. For the life of any one of these I would have gladly given the ship.'

The sinking of *Erin* marked the end – more tragically and more decisively than any other event – of Tommy's golden era. The war had inspired in him a new philanthropy and probably the most selfless actions of his life. It is a tribute to his own courage and speaks volumes about his own true nature that he responded as he did. This wasn't business. This wasn't celebrity. This wasn't a search for public adulation for doing good or saying the right thing, but something more raw and heartfelt. Tommy was responding to his deepest instincts – to act, to do the right thing, to get the job done.

Before the war ended he was focused once more on running his business. He had not forgotten, either, about his other yacht, yet another *Shamrock*, which, having crossed the Atlantic to challenge the NYYC in 1914, had been tied up in New York Harbour since the outbreak of war.

7

Resolute, the fourth challenge, 1920

Long before the bloody and tragic events with which his name would be forever infamously associated, Kaiser Wilhelm was a man who loved sailing, not so much as an innocent pastime, but as a projection of imperial grandeur. The kaiser's yacht, *Hohenzolleren*, weighing in at almost 3,800 tons, was 383 feet long and cost a cool 4.5 million marks to build. Her engines could produce 9,500 horsepower and a speed of 21 knots.

The kaiser also saw yacht racing as an expression of his nation's maritime power. Strange, then, that one of his first manoeuvres was to buy *Thistle*, the defeated 1887 America's Cup challenger of the Royal Clyde Yacht Club. *Thistle* had been skippered by John Barr, the brother of Charlie Barr, who had sailed as mate aboard her. She had been easily defeated by the New York Yacht Club's *Volunteer*, superior in almost every aspect of design and sailing. The kaiser renamed *Thistle*, calling her *Meteor*.

This *Meteor* was re-rigged as a schooner, the first of a series of successful racing *Meteors*. In 1903 and 1904 *Meteor III* was winning races, but the kaiser was never satisfied. He became somewhat jealous of a schooner named *Ingomar*, commanded by the now very experienced and much sought after America's Cup skipper Charlie Barr. *Ingomar* was soon winning races in England and Germany. As Dennis Conner and Michael Levitt have related in their book on the America's Cup, the kaiser commissioned a similar yacht from *Ingomar*'s designer, the prodigious Nathanael Herreshoff. Captain Nat was not unhappy to receive a commission for such a large vessel given the kaiser's deep pockets. He was not so happy, however, when he sent the dimensions of the new yacht to Wilhelm on his request, only to be told to make changes to her draft. Enraged by this interference Herreshoff sent a curt reply and stopped work. The yacht was never built and Kaiser Wilhelm never had his Herreshoff-designed race winner.

Tommy had his own run-in with the kaiser in the same period but, in contrast to Herreshoff, or even Dunraven in the different context of the 1895 America's Cup, he turned the situation around, making it another diplomatic triumph. Tommy had conceived of a transatlantic yacht race between New York and the Isle of Wight. He was ready to put up prize money of $5,000, which, even in this golden age, was generous indeed. Still, it was a serious test of yachting skill and seamanship. Tommy's goal was to stage the race in the summer of 1904. The only problem was that the kaiser had had a similar idea and had sounded out the New York Yacht Club through his American ambassador.

It is again indicative not only of Tommy's sportsmanship but also his sensitivity to the bigger diplomatic stage on which he so much liked to walk, that he backed down, and graciously too. He recognised the potential for embarrassing King Edward and declared that he would be no less than honoured to give the German emperor precedence. Tommy attended Kiel Week and met the emperor there in as cordial and informal an atmosphere as any engagement with Wilhelm would allow. As for the transatlantic race, it was, ironically, postponed in 1904 due to the kaiser's ill health. It was eventually won handsomely in May 1906 by none other than Charlie Barr in the three-masted schooner *Atlantic*. Barr's time for crossing the Atlantic remained unbeaten by any other monohulled yacht until 1997. The cup that he claimed, the one that could so easily have been the Lipton Transatlantic Trophy, was called the Kaiser's Cup.

The Kaiser's Cup may have proved a false start as far as Tommy was concerned, but it was only one of a number of sailing initiatives that he embarked upon in this remarkable post-*Shamrock III* period. Invariably under the name of the Lipton Cup, he inaugurated challenge events between Mississippi steamboats, rowing clubs in Chile, South African yachts from Cape Town, yacht clubs of Tasmania and Victoria, American and Canadian yachts on the Pacific coast, and yachts in the Grand Lakes Boat Race high up in Colorado. Decades before the age of sponsorship and in the earliest days of wireless communication, this is an astonishingly global and varied patronage of sailing competitions. Yet Lipton's ostensible autobiography yields no real clues as to why he committed so much time to this. One biographer, James Mackay, has suggested that at one level he was trying to match the distribution of trophies for all kinds of sports by his friend the whisky baron Tom Dewar, while at another he sought to outdo the Royal Yacht Squadron, making his name synonymous with boating in different forms around the world.

Without clear evidence for his motivation it is only possible to speculate. Certainly these do not seem like the actions of a man calculating commercial gain or seeking world recognition. There is no cohesive strategy behind his sponsorship, and whenever he succumbed to the need to feed his ego, Tommy only had to look to the global ubiquity of the Lipton name and its association with the tea business in so many out-of-the-way places. Neither does it seem likely that he would have been prompted by a desire for rather petty one-upmanship on the Royal Yacht Club at Cowes. He had, after all, witnessed first hand the power of sailing exploits in overcoming personal and political differences on a local, national and international scale. Through his America's Cup challenges at the turn of the century he himself had played no small part in improving Anglo-American relations.

Most likely, he was smitten with both the spirit and fraternity of the sailing community and realised that it presented a multifaceted opportunity — as always with Tommy — to break down barriers of class, community and nationality. His motivations were not about money, selling tea or even besting the Royal Yacht Club. In fact, his actions in the years after this rather eclectic selection of sponsorships — in becalming the German emperor and hosting virtually every royal family of Europe and the American president on board his luxury yacht — suggest that his mind and purpose were more of a social and diplomatic nature.

If there was vanity, arrogance even, involved, it was in his belief that he was Britain's gift to the world. The Royal Yacht Club and its indifference to him were of little consequence when compared with his ambassadorial role on the high seas. There was no person, no matter what blood flowed through their veins, that he couldn't charm, that he couldn't win over. Tommy Lipton at large was good for British interests, representing the acceptable face of Empire. Tommy knew it, as did King Edward, whose patronage he enjoyed. Playing on the ambiguity of his Irish-Scottishness or Scottish-Irishness brilliantly, he rarely lost an opportunity to declare that he was just plain old Tommy Lipton to whomever he met. Considering all that he had achieved, it would perhaps be more surprising if he had not, in less guarded moments, crowed about his own importance.

Over all, in the four-year period following the defeat of *Shamrock III* he ran, in St Benedict's phrase, 'with the light of life'. One minute he was invested as a knight commander of the Order of the Crown of Italy, thanks to his friendship with King Victor Emmanuel II, the next minute he was made an honorary colonel of the Sixth Highland Light Infantry. One day he was announcing another annual dividend of 12 to 15 per cent, another he was popping up in Ceylon to deny speculation he was about to enter the rubber business, or dispose of his meat packing plant interests in Chicago. He always seemed in the right place at the right time whether it was for business, or social engagements with royalty, or even, bizarrely, natural disasters. When Mount Vesuvius erupted in 1906 he was sailing aboard *Erin* in the Mediterranean, and he promptly cruised to Naples to make a contribution to the relief effort. Later, in 1909, when cruising off the Italian coast an earthquake struck Messina and he was yet again soon on the spot, this time with Tom Dewar, to offer assistance.

Whilst Lipton Cups proliferated in the sailing and boating worlds during these consecutive years of global peace across the developed world – with the exception of the Russo-Japanese War of 1904–05 – Tommy's own passion for America's Cup competition was undiminished. In 1907 he was ready to challenge again, but knew that he could not defeat another yacht of such sleek racing dimensions and profile as *Reliance*. Under the rule in which the challenger had to sail across the Atlantic on its own 'bottom', *Reliance* was an outrageous taunt, designed and built to an extreme that no challenger could hope to match. Her only real risk that she was too fragile to withstand persistently inclement racing conditions.

Tommy could not endure another comprehensive defeat like the one inflicted on him by *Reliance* and so in his challenge to the New York Yacht Club in 1907 he proposed that the next challenge be based upon the J Class rating, in use for smaller American racing yachts. J Class yachts had a waterline length of 68 feet and an overall length of 110 feet. Under the current rule the waterline length was 90 feet. *Reliance* at full length was 143 feet, so Tommy's proposal was a significant departure from the norm. *Reliance's* length and size had allowed her designer, the incomparable Nat Herreshoff, to push technology and the science of sailing to the limit. Whereas other designers had struggled to deliver the benefits of scale in terms of steering, weight and the logistics of handling and storing so much canvas, Herreshoff had turned the extra length, additional sail area and weight in the keel to competitive advantage. Tommy regarded Herreshoff as a genius, and he did not doubt that Herreshoff could repeat the feat of 1903. He therefore believed that his only chance of avoiding further humiliation lay in changing the rules to give Herreshoff less scope to demonstrate his wizardry in yacht design.

Unfortunately, from Tommy's perspective, Commodore Ledyard of the New York Yacht Club was quick to dismiss the challenge, arguing in effect that America's Cup racing was about the biggest and the best. J Class yachts, in his view, just didn't have the power or the size to be worthy of the America's Cup, a view endorsed by Pierpont Morgan. In short, if competitors were to race in J Class yachts the status of the America's Cup would be diminished to its detriment. It can be argued that as the defenders of the cup, they were perfectly within their rights, according to the rules, to stipulate the terms of the defence; after all, it should be remembered that it all began with *America* crossing the Atlantic on her own 'bottom' and crushing the cream of British yachts. It can also be argued that, whilst they may have warmed to Sir Thomas over the years, the old guard of the New York Yacht Club had to keep the long-term interests of the cup competition in mind.

With hindsight and from a British perspective, it is easier to argue that in 1907 the great and good of the New York Yacht Club – who were to an extent representative of New York society and the resurgent power and wealth of America as a whole – wasted a chance to reciprocate the sportsmanship shown by Sir Thomas Lipton. They knew better than anyone what he had done to enhance the standing and reputation of the America's Cup in the years following the Dunraven challenge. It was Lipton who had made the cup what it was in the public's eye, not Barr or Herreshoff, or Iselin or Morgan, brilliant men though they all were. The truth was, however, that the cup had become a potent symbol of American strength and technical prowess; it would not be surrendered for sentimental reasons, however endearing to the American people the challenger might be.

In the face of such opposition Tommy had to back down, but he then took the surprising step of commissioning William Fife to build a yacht in the J Class range. She too was to be called *Shamrock* but was not numbered since Tommy wanted to keep the sequence for his actual America's Cup challenges. Built in Dumbarton and launched in 1908 *Shamrock* was one of the finest racing yachts ever to be built on the Clyde. She was an elegant refinement of her predecessors, the America's Cup *Shamrocks*, but was more lavishly constructed, with an interior design of quality hardwoods and tapestries.

This *Shamrock* carried 9,000 square feet of sail canvas, measured 75 feet in length and weighed 175 tons. She could accommodate a crew of twenty-two, including two cooks and two stewards as well as the captain, first and second mates, boatswain, launchman and seamen. Though she was destined to be a racing yacht and to operate primarily in British waters, her design had to incorporate basic living accommodation. For her numbered namesakes that competed in the America's Cup it was no different, given that they had to cross the Atlantic. Alongside her stylish interior decoration, *Shamrock* was the first of the Clyde-built yachts to have electric lighting. As a race yacht she was hard to beat, competing in thirty-five races in the 1908 season around British coasts and taking no less than eleven prizes. Over all, she was to win more than a hundred prizes in British yacht races.

Tommy had not been present at her launch and it is hard to know what his purpose was in commissioning her. Perhaps it was as a spontaneous response to the rejected America's Cup challenge, or a true discovery of sailing, or a way of maintaining his yachting profile in the absence of a foreseeable America's Cup challenge. Perhaps, as seems most likely, it was a mixture of these. Certainly, Tommy had no intention of withdrawing from the America's Cup – he was obsessed with it. Similarly, he had no notion of bowing out of business or public life. From 1908 to 1912 he continued to harangue the New York Yacht Club about a change in the rules to allow for J Class boats. In business he worked long hours in City Road whilst in London, and when abroad he kept in touch by sending a myriad of telegrams. In his public life, he cruised on the *Erin* with the big names and royalty of the day and made sure to attend all the big events, such as London's 1908 Olympic Games. Yet even in the midst of this golden time there were signs that the carefree sweetness of the Edwardian era would soon be replaced by a harsher, more bitter reality for Tommy.

One of the first signals was the arrival of Herbert Asquith as Britain's Liberal prime minister in 1908. His tenure saw significant and far-reaching domestic reforms that were to have a dramatic effect on Britain's social structure and government expenditure. In the so-called 1909 People's Budget of Asquith's Welsh chancellor, Lloyd George, the goal was to raise an additional £16 million to pay for wide-ranging social benefits and a new class of formidable battleships, the dreadnoughts, each capable of 21 knots and carrying ten 12-inch guns – not four as with previous ships. The dynamics of European politics were shifting and Britain needed to put her naval power beyond question.

The rich had to pay most, through new land taxes, new scaled charges for motorcar licences – the bigger the horsepower the bigger the fee – death duties and, not least, a new super tax by which incomes of £5,000 that increased by £3,000 or more were to be taxed 6 pence in the pound. Not surprisingly, the House of Lords rejected the budget, prompting Asquith to call a general election in 1910, which he then won, setting the scene for further Liberal reform. Lloyd George then delivered his National Insurance Act of 1911 by which workers were given better sickness and unemployment insurance provision. The effects on Tommy were twofold: his taxes were rising, as were his costs as an employer. A second signal was a completely unforeseen scandal that made the headlines in 1913 and the opening months of 1914, seriously challenging the good name of Lipton's for the first time ever. Tommy, and Lipton's, had strong links as an army supplier, both Regular and Territorial. Contracts were won and lost on the personal recommendations of senior officers and key people on the ground such as cooks, so the agents of Lipton's had to repeatedly endear themselves to these decision-makers. When one such agent, by the name of Evans, left the company in a salary dispute he decided to publicise the fact that his salary had been used in part as 'expenses', spent in trying to sway the decision-makers. The mist then cleared to reveal that Tommy's employees had been practising widespread bribery of army personnel for years without his knowledge. It was a stark example of how distant Tommy now was from operations and how weak his own management structures and controls were. And for these failings he had no one to blame except himself.

While public and legal retribution were minimal, Tommy keenly felt the discomfort of the affair in his own shareholder meetings. Some were prompted to remark that had he spent less time challenging for an unwinnable cup and gadding about the Mediterranean and more focusing on the details of his business, this sorry episode might never have occurred. For Tommy, while this underlined what he had appre-hended at that first stumbling performance for shareholders in 1898 – that he was no longer his own man – it also represented a shift in their attitude towards him. Up until now, his shareholders had been reason-ably acquiescent as long as the healthy annual dividends were delivered; now they had witnessed his fallibility and were becoming more concerned about their investment.

Mercifully, from Tommy's point of view, his friend, customer and fel-low sailing enthusiast King Edward VII had died in 1910 before the army scandal had gathered momentum. He was succeeded by George V and Queen Mary. Arguably, it was Edward's passing, much more than any of the other clouds gathering on the horizon, that marked the end of Tommy's golden age.

Whatever their relative importance, these signals should have com-bined to make it obvious that it was time for Tommy to step down from his position at the head of Lipton's. However, he had never lost a sense that his mother had handed him the family torch. In spite of her efforts, she had not been able to save her other children, and neither she nor her husband had the drive or the ambition to really make life work. It was up to Tommy, then, to live out the full life that his brothers and sisters had been denied, and to do so with more joie de vivre than either she or her husband had ever felt or experienced. So, irrespective of the warnings signs, Tommy could not let go of the business that he still thought of as his own and his family's. Moreover, Tommy had never really accepted anyone's counsel except his mother's, and there was now no one in his life who was even remotely close enough to be able to suggest retirement to him. And just as he couldn't let go of Lipton's, the America's Cup was his life, his obsession, his dream legacy. Unable to accept that defeat was final, it was time to write to the New York Yacht Club once more.

Whilst the Fife-designed, 23-metre (75 feet) class *Shamrock*, untested by the America's Cup, was winning more silverware for the Lipton collection than any other boat, Tommy continued to press the New York Yacht Club for acceptance of J class boats. Once he stopped asking, making his next challenge unconditional, the august body of men that formed the America's Cup Committee then agreed to the new terms for J class boats in 1913. It was point-scoring of the lowest kind over a man whose openness and sportsmanship was renowned across America. Nevertheless, Tommy was happy: he had the terms he wanted and there was plenty of time to prepare as the challenge was not scheduled until September 1914. He appointed a new designer, Charles Nicholson, a man with a pedigree for building fast boats but who had not been tested in the America's Cup arena. As the authoritative America's Cup commentator and historian John Rousmaniere has noted, this decision had its pros and cons. Nicholson, due to lack of experience in the cup, did not construct his boat to the right specification required by the Universal Rule with the result that the challenger had to cede 7 minutes on handicap to the defender. However, in *Shamrock IV* Nicholson did give Tommy a racing yacht that at long last approached the same levels of technological expertise employed by the Americans.

In stark contrast to the beauty of the unnumbered *Shamrock* designed by Fife, *Shamrock IV* was, as Nicholson himself put it, 'an ugly duckling'. Still, her snub bow and squared-off stern didn't matter because, as Rousmaniere says in his own 1983 history of the America's Cup, 'His boat was built with an ingenuity worthy of Herreshoff, with a spinnaker so light that two men could carry it, several weight-saving devices aloft, a special light air jib, and the first speedometer ever used on a Cup boat.' In short, *Shamrock IV* had innovations that had been so clearly lacking in the earlier *Shamrock*s, making her a genuine contender.

She was constructed in Portsmouth this time, in great secrecy. It was even reported that Tommy insisted that the men who worked on her should all be bachelors so that they didn't go and blab away to their wives about the project. Portsmouth was a spectacular setting for the launch in May of the ugly duckling, which took place amid naval fanfare and gun salutes in honour of Queen Mary's birthday. Tommy, always the showman, was a master of timing and he knew how to throw a party, this time providing lunch for 500 in the boat shed. He had already arranged for 100 photographers and journalists to travel to Portsmouth in a train bedecked with shamrocks. Even the army scandal headlines could not dent his or the media's enthusiasm; over the years he had whipped up such an appetite for the America's Cup in the British public of all social classes that they would have forgiven him anything had he brought back the Auld Mug, and, given his style and graciousness in defeat, they wouldn't have been cheering the win but rather the man who had made it.

Shamrock IV was already underway across the Atlantic when she intercepted a German radio message that announced the commencement of war. After a brief stop in Bermuda, she arrived in New York Harbour, where she would remain in a cradle for nearly six years.

After the grief and desolation of the First World War, the resumption of America's Cup racing in 1920 provided a welcome diversion for nations still coming to terms with their personal and national losses. Other factors also added to the air of excitement. Remarkable though it may seem in this modern era of super-competitive, sponsor-driven sport, there was a genuine desire among many ordinary people in the United States to see Lipton win, and this time he genuinely had a chance. Not only were the yachts J class, as he had wanted, the racing would also take place at New York's Sandy Hook, where racing conditions were less predictable. This would also be the first America's Cup sailed by amateurs, which, in theory at least, made a more even match of the crews. Though it was not known at the time, this was to be the last cup held at Sandy Hook and the last in which handicaps were imposed. It was also to be the last America's Cup raced in gaff-rigged yachts: future yachts would be rigged with triangular, Bermudan mainsails, eliminating the weight and windage of the top-sail spars aloft, making a much more efficient rig.

The team behind the defender was different this time as well. Following Charlie Barr's premature death from a heart attack in Southampton in 1911, his mantle as America's finest sailor had been taken over by Charles Francis Adams, known for his rather formal nature and calmness under pressure. He was consequently known as 'the Deacon' or just 'Deacon'. Born in Quincy, Massachusetts, he had taken his lead from his father, John Quincy Adams, who took him out on fishing trips just outside Boston Harbour. From that humble beginning Charles went on to build and sail race-winning yachts. Outside of his high-powered career in finance, yachting was his only passion. As far back as 1893 he had been helmsman on *Pilgrim* when it competed with *Vigilant* and *Jubilee* for the privilege of defending the America's Cup. Curiously, his most notable victories were won in yachts built and named by him. Each one had seven letters and a double 'o', such as *Baboon*, *Gossoon*, *Papoose*, *Harpoon* and *Rooster*. With these he had success in Germany and Spain.

Not surprisingly, in 1914 the New York Yacht Club elected him as a member. Robert W Emmons, the manager of *Resolute*, the defender, selected him to sail her, and sail her he did with a record of twenty-five victories. By the time of the actual America's Cup of 1920 Adams had skippered *Resolute* – designed by the now ageing, though still incomparable, Herreshoff – in three dazzlingly successful summers. *Resolute*, with the Deacon at the helm, was formidable opposition indeed. *Resolute* was Boston-owned but her crew was mainly Scandinavian by birth. Most, if not all, lived in the United States at that time. The most senior among these was the helmsman Chris Christensen, who had been mate with Charlie Barr. Adams's relationship with Christensen stretched back to 1893 when the latter had been quartermaster on *Pilgrim*. Then, Christensen had attracted Adams's attention and approval by going out on to the gaff in the middle of a race – a dangerous position to be in – and fastening a sail that had become loose. Also on board as navigator was George Nichols, a son-in-law of Pierpont Morgan.

However impressive *Shamrock IV* may have been with her improved technology and speed, *Resolute* was still the stronger contender. Her designer knew better than anyone else living at that time what America's Cup victory required. Her crew had considerably more match-race experience than *Shamrock IV*'s. But it was her skipper that was really a key differentiating factor. One American correspondent said of Adams, 'No quicker or more nimble man ever trod the deck of a yacht. When he wants facts he does not send a man aloft, he goes himself. He never asks a man to do anything he won't do. The men admire him.'

For all Tommy's desired secrecy at Portsmouth, the fact remained that *Shamrock IV* had been in New York for all to see for almost six years. In contrast to the Deacon, who cloaked his yacht with an air of calm and quiet confidence, Tommy covered his with press, photographers and every ordinary New Yorker that wanted to visit. Astonishingly, up to 35,000 visitors, New Yorkers and Americans generally, went aboard *Shamrock IV* in the match build-up.

Again, it is almost impossible to exaggerate the regard and affection on both sides of the Atlantic for the man once described by the *Boston Journal* as 'so perfect a sportsman'. The contests at the turn of the century had in each case attracted up to half a million spectators respectively, as well as page after page of coverage in *The Times*, *The New York Times* and a host of other papers and magazines, much as the World Cup or Olympics are reported on today. Tommy was himself later to tell of the thousands of mascots that he received. 'The *Erin*'s decks and state rooms were littered with them', he observed. 'At different times I received no fewer than 17 Irish terriers. But I had less difficulty with them than I had with one American eagle which a well-wisher insisted on my accepting for luck.'

If there was a contrast between the measured methodical ambience of *Resolute* and the circus surrounding *Shamrock IV*, there was arguably an even more significant difference between the two skippers, the considered and phlegmatic Adams and, by all accounts, the moody and temperamental Sir William Burton. Burton fitted Tommy's criterion for hiring the best available and there was no dispute that he was Britain's best amateur skipper at the time. However, as it would turn out, his character and judgement were at times open to question.

To start with, Burton had insisted that his wife, an experienced yachtswoman, be a member of the crew of *Shamrock IV*. This was poorly judged, because it put the crew ill at ease. Quite apart from the fact that she was the captain's wife this was due, in some measure, to long-established maritime superstitions which held that women at sea brought bad luck. Taken together, then, in the mind of the crew there were issues of competence, distraction and favouritism. Tommy could have stepped in and prevented Burton's selection of his wife, and it was a mistake that he didn't do so, but he did not wish to undermine Burton or cause any more anxiety over what was already a disrupted match. Admittedly, dismissing Burton before the first race in the series would also have made him look both foolish and indecisive, surely dimming the glow of media coverage that he had come to enjoy. Interestingly, Burton's crew were Essex fishermen, good enough at handling boats and difficult weather conditions, but not nearly as practised as the race-hardened crew they were going to face. For better or for worse, then, the stage was set for the thirteenth match of the America's Cup in July 1920.

On 15 July a sea of spectator craft and patrol boats awaited the scheduled 1 p.m. start. A 30-mile, two-leg course had been set, with the first leg running into the wind up to the windward mark. The two crews jousted for the best position in the invisible boxed arena behind the starting line, their goals to manoeuvre into a space ahead of their opponent so that they had the advantage of crossing the start line first; to force their opponent, if possible, into the mistake of crossing the start line ahead of the scheduled time, thus incurring a penalty; and to pick the side of the course on which the wind would be most in their favour. In these tense, technical pre-start minutes the yachts swooshed so close to each other that the crews were almost eyeball to eyeball, the tactics of each clearly visible to the other, the shouted instructions of the helmsman almost audible above the spray.

No penalties were incurred in this first duel, though, as *Resolute* took the advantage over the line and held it in light rain. Not yet up to the windward mark, *Shamrock IV* was now 5 minutes behind – 12 minutes in reality because of her handicap – when disaster struck. But for once it wasn't the challenger's disaster: the line used to haul aloft the upper front corner of *Resolute*'s giant four-sided mainsail, the throat halyard, suddenly snapped, causing the gaff – the spar that supported the top edge of the mainsail – to come down off the mast. The situation was irretrievable. Though Burton discussed with his afterguard – navigator, tactician, helmsman – whether he should call the race off, the simple fact was that America's Cup racing was as much about preparation and the endurance of the boat as it was about actual racing. *Resolute* failed to finish, and on this, his fourth attempt to win the America's Cup, Tommy won his first race. Some luck was on his side at last.

On 20 July a 30-mile course again awaited the contestants, but this time it comprised three legs of equal distance. Adams and his crew wanted revenge, having been cheated by circumstance out of their first race victory. In the duel that unfolded, with both boats sailing across the wind for each of the three legs, the breeze was just, though only just, strong enough to allow *Shamrock IV* to hold her speed and leave *Resolute* in her wake. She held the advantage and crossed the line more than 9 minutes ahead of *Resolute*. Time adjusted, she won by 2 minutes and 22 seconds.

It was too good to be true. On no less than nine previous occasions, surrounded by his expectant guests on *Erin*, Tommy had watched a *Shamrock* humbled by the defender, while he quickly scanned his mental phrase book on defeat for an appropriately sportsmanlike or witty remark. This time, on the *Victoria*, he could hardly contain himself as the waiting fleet of spectator boats rent the New York air with whistles, sirens and hooters. He could not resist the temptation at this point to order a special case in which the cup could be safely placed for its return to Britain. Even so, Tommy knew that his two victories were lucky, in the sense that one was achieved through his opponent's misfortune and the other was won almost by luck in the lightest of winds. *Resolute* had almost stolen a race between times, but pathetic winds prevailed and she failed to finish on time. Tommy wanted victory from skill and racing speed.

From the July 21 starting line at Ambrose Channel Lightship a 15-mile run to the windward mark and back again was all that stood between *Shamrock IV* and cup victory. She needed a clean start and the right decision on which side of the course would have the most favourable wind, but this time the cool Adams took *Resolute* to a small lead of 19 seconds from the start. Burton tacked again and again, turning the bow of *Shamrock IV* into the wind in an effort to reach the windward mark ahead of the defender, but Adams brought *Resolute* round the mark first with a lead of 2 minutes for the homeward stretch.

The lead was short-lived, however: as *Shamrock IV* rounded the

mark, her spinnaker set, her sails full, she hunted down *Resolute* relentlessly as both boats sailed downwind to the finishing line. The extra sail
area that *Shamrock IV* paid for with a 7-minute handicap was now giving her the additional speed she needed. *Resolute* could not hold her
off, and Burton and his crew caught and sailed beyond the defender.
Shamrock IV crossed the finish line. The seconds passed. With one last
surge of speed Adams hauled *Resolute* over the line 19 seconds after
Shamrock IV. It was enough, in fact much more than enough, on cor-
rected time, though in actual racing time it was a dead heat because
Shamrock IV had crossed the starting line exactly 19 seconds behind
Resolute. Although to the untrained eye the race had appeared very
close, the defender had won this match comfortably. Still, *Resolute*
would have to beat *Shamrock IV* twice more if she was to keep the cup
in American hands.

It was after this third race that Tommy was quoted in *The New York
Times* as saying, 'The victory of the *Resolute* means that we have a good
fight on our hands which is just what I want. It means that we have a
good opponent in this race. Three straight victories is something
which never appealed to me.'

On 23 July *Shamrock IV* was still just 30 miles away, this time on a
triangular course, from winning the America's Cup for the Royal
Ulster Yacht Club. *Resolute*, the white defender, was first across the line,
at 1:01:33. *Shamrock IV*, the green-hulled challenger, followed her at
1:01:56. She looked in good shape, and the change in the step of her
mast — slightly forward, increasing the angle of its rake back towards
the stern — was helping her as she sailed into the wind. She quickly
caught up to the defender, her course closer to *Resolute*'s at the start
than in their previous encounters. In a 6-knot breeze, with the wind
blowing over the starboard side, Burton brought *Shamrock IV* about so

that she was pointing in shore towards Sandy Hook, now with the wind on her port side. It was an early gamble, made in the belief that *Shamrock IV* would pick up a stronger breeze. Meanwhile, Adams held his line southwards, benefiting from streaks of wind that propelled the defender on towards the first mark, now only 8 miles away. Burton's risk didn't pay off: the breeze dropped for him and for tense moments it looked almost as though *Shamrock IV* was heading back to the line.

Resolute now had the advantage. Little more than 12 minutes after the start the charging white defender was a quarter of a mile to windward of *Shamrock IV*. She had good heel, the whole yacht being tilted over due to the pressure of the wind on her sails. *Resolute*, in contrast, on her southward heading, had the advantage. The breeze increased to 10 knots. Crashing through the water *Resolute* had the momentum, now putting up the three-sided headsail known as the jib topsail to boost her speed. In contrast, *Shamrock IV* was struggling on her shore-bound course. She could not sustain any speed and at 2 p.m. Burton headed her off shore. This brought *Shamrock IV* up through the lee of the defender but there was virtually no gain. For the remainder of the run to the windward mark *Shamrock IV* chased the stern of *Resolute* but made little impact on her lead.

Resolute turned at the windward mark and continued to keep the by now very frustrated Burton and his crew astern. Changing wind conditions after a brief thunder squall made it difficult for both crews to choose the right sails. Word leaked out after the race that a sense of desperation took hold of Burton and his afterguard as they tried different sail combinations, anything, as they sailed across wind, that would put them out in front. Their efforts were all in vain. *Resolute* crossed the line at 3:37:52. *Shamrock IV* followed at 3:41:40. It was only a matter of minutes, but an eternity in America's Cup racing, where a difference

of more than 40 seconds is considered a big margin. With the handicap for her sails taken into account, the margin of defeat in this fourth
contest was a significant 9 minutes and 58 seconds.

Prospects were not looking good for the challenger. The shifting
wind conditions in the fourth race had betrayed a weakness in Burton's
decision-making in the choice of sail. Approaching the mark with a
lead of 2 minutes and 12 seconds, *Resolute*'s baby jibtopsail was taken
down less than one minute before the buoy was reached. The jibtopsail was drawn out as she made the turn. The *Shamrock IV* crew, in
sharp contrast, was much slower: she was fully three minutes past the
buoy before number one jibtopsail was drawing.

In addition to this, during *Shamrock IV*'s second leg more than 4
minutes elapsed between the taking down of the first jibtopsail and the
trimming down of a second. Worst of all, when the wind increased in
that second leg from 12 to 18 knots – conditions in which the ocean-
going and more robust challenger was thought to excel – she could
not cut down the lead of the superbly handled defender by even half.
By the second turn *Shamrock IV* had gained only 57 seconds. With the
series tied at 2–2, the wind had, quite literally, gone out of *Shamrock
IV*'s sails and the pendulum had swung back in the defender's favour.
The next pre-start tacking and gybing duel would decide the series.

Racing yachts that are 75 feet at the waterline and have sails that
reach some 100 feet up into the sky in the wind of 25 knots would be
a dangerous and foolhardy activity – Adams and Burton both knew
that. But on 24 July, in conditions more akin to the wild open ocean,
Tommy could only see a perfect race day to overcome a more sleek
and fragile defender. Adams and Burton agreed with the committee
that racing should be aborted for that day. Tommy had not been consulted by Burton and, in the heat of the moment, protested bitterly and

uncharacteristically, accepting only later that the correct decision had been taken.

What galled him most was that Burton had not consulted him. Though not a yachtsman, Tommy was astute enough to know from his own observations and from the cumulative wisdom of the yachting sages all around him that Burton was not getting the best from his crew. There was too much debate in the afterguard and the initial aggravation caused by Burton selecting his wife as a crew member was not abating.

If winning the America's Cup, his life obsession, hadn't meant so much to him, Tommy might have been struck by the irony of the whole situation. With Burton he had won two more races than with Hogarth, Wringe or Sycamore. Yet in Burton he could also seen a major obstacle to *Shamrock IV* bringing home the Auld Mug to Britain. Only another stroke of luck or an unexpected turn of events in the final race could prove him wrong.

On 25 July far fewer spectator craft witnessed the arrival of *Resolute* and *Shamrock IV* in the tactical arena behind the starting line. Though the stakes had not changed, this contest had become a long, drawn-out affair bedevilled by the capricious moods of the New York coastal winds. Only the committed yachtsmen were out in force in the Ambrose Channel to see whether *Shamrock IV* was capable of regaining momentum and winning the cup.

But the agonising wait, for competitors and onlookers alike, was not over yet, as the gun to signal the start of the race at 12 p.m. was not fired. What little breeze there had been had died away. A postponement at 15-minute intervals, automatically renewed, was ordered. And all the while, the tension and the waiting had to be contained. Sails empty, the two gladiators turned in slow, creaking, intersecting circles, each crew member watching for weakness on an opposite number's face as the yachts crept around each other, each alert to a sudden change in wind conditions, always ready to seize the tactical advantage.

By 2 p.m. the wind speed had built up to 3 knots. Bang! At 2.15, the deciding match of the thirteenth America's Cup – a 15-mile run to the windward mark, south by south-west from the starting line down the New Jersey coast, and then home – was underway at last. But the anticlimactic feeling that pervaded this duel fought in slow motion continued as neither *Shamrock IV* nor *Resolute* could cross the line within two minutes of the starting signal. So, even though *Shamrock IV* eventually crossed the line a full 40 seconds ahead of *Resolute*, this advantage counted for nothing: they were credited by the committee as having both crossed the line at the same time.

To the uninformed eye, it really did look as though the challenger was making the most of the weak wind conditions after half an hour's sailing. Burton had done well to keep her on the edge of the wind, keeping her several hundred yards ahead of the defender. Her lead continued to extend to nearly half a mile. Yet, as is so often the case in the America's Cup, both then and now, appearances can be very deceptive. It was in this second half hour of racing that Adams found a better slant of wind, enabling him to point *Resolute* into the wind higher than *Shamrock IV*, thus reducing her lead. Now much closer together, the two wavering, white-sailed boats made several tacks. *Shamrock IV* couldn't resist, and just 3 miles short of the windward mark *Resolute* was able to cross the challenger's bow and place herself, as yachtsmen say, on her opponent's weather. In effect this meant that as the wind began to pick up, *Resolute* was in the position to benefit from it first.

Resolute rounded the mark more than 4 minutes ahead of *Shamrock*

IV. Within 30 seconds of doing so, she had her balloon jib sail set, billowing out in front of her down the homeward leg. It is telling of the difference between the two crews and their leadership that *Shamrock IV*'s balloon jib was only set to catch the downwind a full 2 minutes after rounding the mark.

Both *Resolute* and *Shamrock IV* gybed twice in the first 5 miles of the 15-mile run to the finish. *Resolute* held her advantage in the light air and led by nearly a mile after an hour's sailing before the wind on this homeward leg. *Shamrock IV* was doomed. Her only hope was that the wind, now freshening to 6 knots, would drop dramatically again, preventing *Resolute* from completing the course on time.

And with only 4 miles and less than an hour of allotted time to go for *Resolute*, the wind did drop. Might *Shamrock IV* just possibly live to fight another day? Not for the first time this duel appeared to be happening in slow motion. As the minutes ticked and *Resolute* inched towards the finish line, hopes for Shamrock *IV* began to dwindle. The defender crossed the line with 24 minutes to spare before the time limit was exceeded. *Shamrock IV*, handicap and all, was beaten. In classic Lipton style, Tommy commanded the captain of his own yacht, *Victoria*, to sail down to *Resolute* after she had crossed the finishing line and, led by Tommy, all hands and all guests on board gave her three rousing cheers. *Shamrock IV* was still a mile away on the course.

In the moment of defeat, there would be no excuses from Tommy, no public reprimand for William Burton, or his crew or for *Shamrock IV*'s designer, Charles Nicholson. It was by now a well-practised Lipton routine to offer unconditional and heartfelt congratulations to the victors, to tell all and sundry that the best boat had won and to declare that he would not give up on his dream of winning the America's Cup just yet. Neither do his memoirs point a belated finger at any of the *Shamrock IV* team, including himself. Paradoxically, herein lies his great strength and weakness. He could take defeat on the chin in a manner arguably unparalleled in sport before or since. He could stand up and look forward to the next challenge. The words 'if only' never crossed his lips. Yet, by the same measure he was incapable of expressing remorse, of admitting that he got it wrong, of learning from his mistakes. No one man or woman – not forgetting Mrs Burton – can win or lose the America's Cup, but it is hard to escape the conclusion that Tommy's weaknesses and poor judgement were more cruelly exposed in the 1920 challenge than any other. For, whilst it is true to say that *Shamrock I, II* and *III* were all soundly beaten, *Shamrock IV* is the one that actually lost the America's Cup. There is a difference.

In *Shamrock IV* Tommy had a yacht brimming with innovation and technological advances compared with other yachts of pre-war British design. In Charles Nicholson, chief naval architect of the firm Camper & Nicholson, he had found a designer of exceptional talent who, unlike Herreshoff, was an experienced and accomplished sailor who knew how to motivate and direct a boat's crew. As the *Philadelphia Enquirer* noted when the speculation over Burton's continuing captaincy was at its height, 'Nicholson is a skilled helmsman which he demonstrated several times when he took the wheel in trials.'

However, six years elapsed between *Shamrock IV*'s launch and her first America's Cup match. She had little race practice or tuning up of any sort. Her predominantly Essex-based crew, a number of whom had been transferred from Tommy's non-America's Cup *Shamrock*, only boarded *Shamrock IV* for the first time in July 1920, the month of the first scheduled race. Like *Shamrock IV*'s crew of forty, Burton had a CV that demonstrated he had more than ample experience, but he didn't know *Shamrock IV*, he had no special rapport with Tommy Lipton and he was no match for the battle-hardened Adams who knew how *Resolute* would handle and what sail or manoeuvre was required for maximum speed in almost every conceivable racing condition.

So why didn't Tommy wake up to the fact that *Shamrock IV* was headed for defeat? Was he so seduced by the innovations and design improvements of *Shamrock IV*? Had he not taken into account the number of race wins notched up by Adams on *Resolute*? And why did he not substitute Burton when he had the chance with the man who knew the handling of *Shamrock IV* far better than any and, it would seem, commanded more respect among the crew, namely her designer, Charles Nicholson? Some answers to this last question have already been suggested, but added to these might be Burton's own plea to Tommy when press speculation was mounting. In a private exchange Sir William implored Tommy to give him his chance, saying he had not yet had full opportunity to show his skills.

Nicholson's gushing admission of his own contribution to errors made in the first two races also let Lipton's embattled captain off the hook: 'I was responsible for the bad start of *Shamrock* in the first race', he said. He confirmed that he had recommended to Burton the employment of a large jibtopsail in going to windward. He went on to dilute the criticism of the captain: 'Burton may have been a little off his game on Saturday. All captains have good and bad days. Burton was possibly put off by too many suggestions, especially my own. There's only room for one captain.'

Nicholson was right. A boat should only have one captain and it should have been him. His own confession and loyalty to Burton were misplaced atonement for errors in the first races. By replacing Burton with Nicholson after the second race Tommy would have immediately eased the tension in the crew and instilled new confidence, for Mrs Burton, who only ever sailed with her husband, would have also left. Burton's indecisiveness in debating strategy with his afterguard at key moments would also have been removed, thus giving a boost to Tommy's chances of winning that elusive third race.

As it was, there was broad consensus in the press among yachting experts that a combination of poor morale and bad handling was *Shamrock IV*'s downfall and not, most notably, her racing speed. 'Captain Burton has clearly shown that he is not familiar with his charge, that in certain tight corners he is not sure just what the yacht will do', reported the *Boston Globe*. And again, it was widely reported in the American press after racing began that 'the crew of the *Shamrock* were on the verge of mutiny on account of the presence aboard of the skipper's wife, namely Mrs Burton, who is acting as timekeeper'. This quote appeared in many British newspapers.

When the fate of the cup was finally decided in *Resolute*'s favour, even the British press, which had remained prone to sniping at American defenders, describing them variously as light weather yachts, or 'mere shells', were gracious in complimenting *Resolute*'s predominantly Scandinavian crew, led by Christensen, under Adams.

Who can say now whether putting Nicholson at the helm of *Shamrock IV* for the final three matches would have resulted in British victory and a very different legacy for Sir Thomas Lipton? Who can say whether any combination of sails and leadership could have overcome over five races such a well-drilled and professional outfit as Adams had put together? What can be said with the benefit of nearly ninety years' hindsight is that Tommy Lipton himself must take the blame for not finding out.

Tommy approached this cup as he had all the rest: he carefully considered the appointment of the designer and skipper and then let them get on with the job. From then on, he played the role of performer in his own familiar media circus. The press interviews, the publicised visits to the boatyard to check on progress, the high society engagements, the extravagant launch were all a well-practised routine. It was a routine, however, that meant more to him that ever before. After the horrors of the war that had preceded it, he genuinely wanted this America's Cup to be a great celebration for all interested countries. Personally, since his own war experiences in Serbia, the last few years had been rewarding enough in business but monotonous and unexciting. The only major development had been the move in August of Lipton's Tea United States Head Office from a small suite of offices in New York's Franklin Street to a twelve-storey building at Hoboken. Every boat coming up the Hudson now saw the Lipton's Tea sign.

Tommy's turnover in America had been increasing steadily, due in no small part to prohibition, and overall Lipton's was sustaining its 12 per cent dividend. Tommy himself had been more home-based in the immediate postwar years, spending long days at the office in London and returning to Osidge late at night, where he would frequently browse through his large collection of press-cutting albums. Although the fact that he had no family had spared him the tragedy of losing loved ones in the First World War, it also excluded him from the joy of reunion. In the period 1917 to 1920 he seems a rather isolated and lonely figure, and it was must have been hard, even for him, not to look back wistfully and brood. As the cup approached, however, his time had come to be reunited with his adopted family – the America's Cup fraternity. Dressed in blue jacket, spotted bow tie, white flannels and yachting cap, and with the Lipton flag – a green shamrock on a field of gold – raised aloft, Sir Thomas Lipton, Vice Commodore of the

Royal Ulster Yacht Club, was ready to receive guests on board the *Victoria*. On 18 July alone, Tommy played host to Henry Ford, whose own yacht, *Sialia*, has just anchored in New York, Sir Tom Dewar, Sir John and Lady Ferguson and the daughters of Lord Inverforth, Misses Nita and Ella Weir.

In the midst of all this entertaining Tommy did, of course, keep time aside each day, usually around dusk, for a team conference to discuss *Shamrock IV*'s strategy. The truth is, though, that Tommy was on his own America's Cup autopilot, and he would not risk spoiling the party, nor making himself look disloyal or foolish, by dismissing Burton. *Shamrock IV* was a fast ugly duckling with enough speed to defeat *Resolute*, Adams's excellent seamanship and crew notwithstanding, but in 1920 Tommy Lipton made the wrong decisions. He lost the America's Cup.

8

Lipton logs the final decade

Embellished with shamrock sprigs and two shields with the inter-twined letters TJL emblazoned upon them, the two 8-foot tall, heavy, green iron gates swung open to let Tommy's 1910 Mercedes pass through. With goggles on and car loaded up, he swung left and up Chase Side, accelerating out of Southgate. His destination on that bright Sunday morning in July 1921 was Cooper's Green in Hertfordshire, some 15 miles away.

Apart from his First World War endeavours and the America's Cup campaign of the previous year, Tommy had been at home in Southgate on many a Sunday in the preceding seven years. This Sunday excursion, then, as with so much else in his life, had become a habit, a ritual almost. Throughout the 1920s, as he moved through his seventies, these habits would become more pronounced as he clung to what was familiar in friends, business and daily routine. He had no financial worries and continued to live in good health and in a degree of luxury available to only a few in postwar Britain.

Yet, ironically, it was his very good fortune that isolated him and put him out of step with the changed attitudes and values of a postwar world. In *The Lipton Story*, Alec Waugh argues unconvincingly that the 1920s should have been the perfect decade in Lipton's life: 'He had entered, it seemed, upon a happy and tranquil autumn. His life's work lay behind him. His achievements lay before his eyes . . . and always the hope that one day he would see a *Shamrock* coming home first at Sandy Hook. That last decade should have been . . . at least the most satisfying of his life'. Only a 1920 victory over *Resolute*, however, would have made that so, giving him a glow of achievement to carry through the decade. For the truth about the other passion of his life, his business, was that it had attained a size and complexity that could not be controlled by his own management methods or the philosophy on which business had been based. Comparisons of the accounts and reports of the directors from 1920 onwards show this to be true.

In 1917 and 1918 the company had performed better than at any time since 1908, overcoming constraints imposed by the wartime food controller. In 1918 net profits were up 44 per cent and the highest ever dividend, 12.5 per cent, was approved – the dividend of 11 per cent between 1898 and 1900 having been the previous record. It is interesting to note that not even at the peak of Tommy's allegedly profit- and publicity-driven America's Cup campaigns of 1900 to 1904 did the business deliver bigger dividends than these. If their sole intention had been to dramatically increase profit through a unique means of attracting publicity in the United States, in other words a plotted business strategy, then they most surely did not deliver the transformational results expected.

The 'Directors' Report' for 1918 intimated that Lipton's progress had been made possible by the reorganisation of the business and an increase in trade. The expansion continued, but even so shareholders at the annual general meeting in July 1919 wanted to know whether the company's shops were being operated at a profit and whether there was any truth in recent rumours that this part of the business was to be absorbed by a well-known catering company. They would have been well aware of the intense and consolidating competition in the high street that had, since the turn of the century, seen large-scale food retailers' share of the market increase from 11 per cent to nearly 20 per cent. Lipton's shareholders had heard the rumours at the beginning of 1919 about a possible partnership or merger that would impact on their business and returns. Speculation focused on two companies, Lyons and the ABC Company, the former an operator of the new 'tea' shops – that is, those that served tea – and the latter a more traditional catering company.

The finance column of the *Outlook* in February 1919 neatly summed up a widely held view in the market: 'There can be no doubt that a combine between two or three of the present competitors in this line would make for mutual strength and economy. For years past rivalry has been intense and wasteful. Shops have been opened side by side wherever likely premises were available, irrespective of the prospects of the divided custom being profitable to either party. In many instances the result being the reverse of profitable.' Tommy, however, was not persuaded of the merits of this perspective. On the basis of almost fifty years of successful trading, he simply believed the public would always love Lipton's. He could blame the absence of a dividend in 1915 and 1916 on the exceptional circumstances of the war, and Lipton's postwar increase in trade amply demonstrated that the public would always respond to high-quality tea and groceries at the lowest possible prices. Not only that, as Tommy reported at this

1919 annual general meeting, more new branches had been opened in Britain as well as in Jaffa, in Haifa in Syria and in Shoubra, a suburb of Cairo. Further expansion at home and abroad was planned and, in conclusion, Tommy was 'personally convinced that the business, although established more than 40 years ago is only in its infancy'. Applause. He left the question of amalgamation to his deputy chairman, C Williamson Milne, who said that there was 'no amalgamation afoot . . . as far as Lipton's was concerned'. In fact, such confidence in future growth and independence was entirely misplaced and betrayed a complacency, an arrogance even, that emanated directly from Tommy himself.

However, on the surface business seemed to be going well. The passing of the Prohibition Amendment in the United States by Congress in December 1917 and its ratification in January 1919 came as a surprise: 'Prohibition could not come in England', he observed, 'and it is with great amazement that I see that you . . . have passed the amendment providing that a man shall not drink certain things. In England we have always imagined Americans as being the freest people on earth and as being most jealous of that freedom.' Still, it was a business opportunity, and Tommy initiated a $250,000 advertising campaign, run in 175 newspapers across the United States. Carrying the slogan 'A Million Dollars for a Cup of Tea', the full-page adverts told the story of a tea planter's determination to give the world the perfect cup of tea.

Coinciding as this did with another America's Cup challenge and the move to larger, more prominent office and warehousing at Hoboken in New Jersey, the timing of the campaign was perfect from Tommy's point of view. This was not a 'happy and tranquil autumn': Tommy was fired up once more. Though the foundation of his business empire was not nearly as firm as he supposed, it is a mark of his remarkable appetite for life that in an era when people expected little activity from men in their seventies Tommy was striding out once more, not yet tired of challenging America in business as well as on the water. As the caption of his speech to his employees in the American adverts said, 'I want the best tea that can be produced. If you have to spend a million dollars to get it, do so. Remember, the best tea and nothing short of that. Nothing else counts!'

Yet, like everything else in the company, these very words had to be approved by him. Tommy had appointed four other directors of the company before 1920, but this had by no means created a strong collegiate decision-making body that would challenge his assertions. Alfred Bowker, an eminent lawyer and future mayor of Winchester, was one of the board. Only a few weeks after his Sunday drive to Cooper's Green, in August 1921, Tommy was Alfred Bowker's best man for his wedding to Miss Brett. He then became godfather to their first son. In short, Tommy and Alfred Bowker were close friends. Though long-serving – he remained on the board up to 1926 – Bowker's voice was not of the critical or dissenting variety. Nor was there continuity on the board: deputy chairman C Williamson Milne left due to ill health, spending his healthy time managing his own business.

In his desire to control every aspect of the business, Tommy held up the launch of Lipton's Coffee on the American market in 1922 by insisting on endless experiments in blending and then the resolution of the problem of finding packaging that kept the coffee fresh. The vacuum tins were not satisfactory and eventually a tin with a screw-lock device was found, but Tommy's insistence on being directly involved and personally satisfied cost valuable time and money. As ever, the American press was complimentary, admiring his 'characteristic thoroughness', but in reality he had not delegated well enough or trusted his managers sufficiently to resolve the problems more quickly. Given that roasting and packing plants had already been set up in New York, Chicago, San Francisco and New Orleans, these were costly delays. This one development is indicative, too, of both the headlong rush for expansion abroad and the new complexities of the business.

However, it was not just the one-man decision-making structure that made this globally tentacled business so vulnerable in the culturally different 1920s: Lipton's was imbued with a social conscience that seriously impaired its capacity to make profit and ultimately to function in a more competitive, commercially driven environment. As a boy and young man Tommy had witnessed the hardships of poverty and the unforgiving nature of a state that provided no safety net. By making the essentials of life affordable, he was throwing a lifeline to many; what was the right thing to do also made business sense – it was corporate social responsibility in its purest form. He exceeded the expectations of his customers and his staff stakeholders and, more, he earned their heartfelt gratitude.

The comments in the 'Report of the Directors' in 1920 are typical of every report that preceded it: 'Goods have been sold at the same low rate of profit as in previous years . . . the large increase in home trade bears striking testimony to the popularity of the branches and the soundness of the policy of selling goods of the best quality at the smallest possible margin of profit.' The difference now, however, was that expenditure had risen considerably. In addition, as the 1921 report stated, there were 'unprecedented falls in market values of commodities dealt in by the company'. At home there were strikes and high unemployment whilst 'adverse markets and unsatisfactory world conditions' deprived Lipton's of much-needed revenue. Neither the company's expansion nor its boast of aiming for a low profit margin were looking too clever by the summer of 1921. Prices had not been increased because it was against stated company policy, in other words Tommy's principles.

In a May interview Tommy declared that yes, he had seen conditions as bad as these before, and he reminisced about when the City Bank in Glasgow had failed. In his 'softly, softly' way he vented his frustration that the unemployed of today tended to blame others. But his optimism that the 'tide will turn' and provide an opportunity 'for those who bring to their tasks enthusiasm, energy and wit' sounded hollow in the context of his own company's structure and outlook.

Perhaps Tommy was blinded by his own vain view of himself. He certainly could not see that factors in the external environment had multiplied to such a degree that he could not possibly expect to influence them, and he did not accept that he could not go on for ever and take steps to secure the company's future. In that regard an 'amalgamation' with Lyons would have been a natural step to take, but it was a step that Tommy either couldn't see or couldn't take. The similarities and contrasting fortunes of the two businesses provide a useful insight into Tommy's shortcomings. At the same time as Tommy was revolutionising the way in which tea was bought and sold, another business extrovert was expanding the tea market in a manner that had previously been unthinkable. His name was Joey Lyons and the innovation that made his a household name was the opening of a chain of teashops.

Though Joey did not own the Lyons business as Tommy Lipton did his, there were nevertheless similarities in his approach to running it. Firstly, his product appealed to customers because it was markedly different and so obviously better than the offerings of competitors: his teashops were bright, well lit, well ventilated and spotlessly clean; fresh flowers in vases sat on top of pristine white tablecloths and waitresses were polite and smartly dressed. Like Tommy, Joey also concentrated on price: the going rate for a cup of tea was three pence at the time, but Joey opted to serve the best tea at twopence a pot. As more shops were opened Joey Lyons kept to a practice of charging the same for a cup of tea in each, regardless of location – a shrewd move that further enhanced his reputation. The similarities to Lipton in business ethics and approach were uncanny. Like Lipton, Joey Lyons even won the backing of the future Edward VII, who was known to remark, 'I like Mr Lyons. He feeds my people well.' And, like Lipton, Mr Lyons received his knighthood.

Joey's teashops became a foundation for even greater success, with Lyons becoming one of the four dominant tea brands in Britain in the last century, the other three being Brooke Bond, Co-op and Typhoo. These four flourished through a growing number of new outlets, driven by distribution and advertising. In 1970, fifty-three years after Joey Lyons himself had died from Bright's disease, the Lyons business had a turnover of nearly £130 million, sold almost 40 per cent of all the ice cream eaten in Britain, had captured more than 20 per cent of the frozen food market and continued to hold a chain of teashops. Lyons did not last as an independent business, but it certainly outlived and outperformed Lipton's. The Lyons white-and-gold teashops became a much loved part of the British high street landscape, and the immaculately turned out red-dressed Lyons waitresses, who became known as Nippies, were a regular sight at all major events as well as in the teashops themselves.

Fundamentally, the difference between the two men, Lyons and Lipton, was that Lyons was not ultimately responsible for the big decisions. J Lyons the business was not cast in the image of Joey Lyons to the same degree that Lipton's was a mirror of Tommy Lipton. If Joey had survived the First World War and remained active in business he is unlikely to have struggled in the way that Tommy Lipton did with the profit expectations, the changes in management style needed to adjust to the postwar culture and the realisation that the golden carefree Edwardian era really was over. Even if he had, it wouldn't have mattered because the Salmon & Gluckstein families held the reins of power and saw the opportunity to extend the Lyons brand and to work with other suppliers in the wholesale and retail trade. In contrast, Tommy Lipton focused on his own retail outlets, where he would only stock Lipton's Tea. Roy Moxham in his book *Tea Addiction, Exploitation and Empire* is in no doubt about Tommy's error and the gradual disappearance of Lipton's stores after his death: 'Lipton's major mistake was to concentrate on his own retail shops. He opened over 600, but other shopkeepers saw this as competition and opted to stock other brands. Sales withered away, Lipton's own shops began to close because of bad management and the Lipton name slowly disappeared in Britain.'

Long after the demise of Joey Lyons, successive generations of Salmons and Glucksteins expanded and diversified, and by 1977 group sales worldwide had reached £790 million. However, J Lyons & Co. was in serious trouble with mounting debt and significant losses in the UK business. In 1978 Allied Breweries bought the company, the various brands were sold off, and J Lyons & Co disappeared. Even though J Lyons & Co was undoubtedly a better run, more sustainable business, and one that outlived Lipton's by fifty years, it is ironic that it is Lipton Tea that remains a global brand in the first decade of the twenty-first century, while the Lyons brands, from teashops to ice cream, are only a memory. The Lipton brand, acquired by Unilever in the early 1970s, is available in most countries of the world with sales calculated in billions of pounds.

As Tommy sped, and it is almost inconceivable that he wasn't speeding, towards Cooper's Green on that summer Sunday in July 1921, the children were waiting for him, as usual. Almost seven years ago he had driven through the village of Cooper's Green and noticed two little girls playing in their garden by the road. He had stopped to speak to them, giving them a box of chocolates each from his car. He had promised to return again with more chocolates another Sunday. And so he had, Sunday after Sunday, year after year. Whenever he was at home he drove to Cooper's Green laden with chocolates for the two girls and all the children of the village. Any guests staying with him were obliged to make this weekly pilgrimage and ritual, a ritual that also included giving all the children a ride in his car. On this particular Sunday, though, the children and their mothers expressed their love and thanks by presenting him with an oak frame containing an earlier picture taken of him and the children together on his car. It would not be the last tribute he received in the 1920s.

These trips to Cooper's Green were just a fraction of Tommy's total philanthropy. In 1921 he gave his usual $500 to the New York Children's Christmas Fund, but he reserved his large gifts for the poor in Britain. In December 1922 he made the remarkable gesture of donating parcels worth a total of £100,000 to families most in need. Tommy himself turned up in Glasgow to help distribute them at Christmas. Each parcel contained tea, cocoa, sugar, flour, currants, raisins, rice and condensed milk. He had recruited a staff of 200 unemployed people to pack 4,000 cases.

In January 1923 he was at it again. This time the beneficiaries were more than a thousand poor children of Finsbury and Shoreditch who he entertained at the Leysian Mission on City Road close to his head-quarters. For this Saturday-evening event he employed the goodwill and services of his fellow directors and employees, the latter forming the Lipton Choral Society.

An accumulation of a lifetime's generosity and outstanding achieve-ments in business were duly recognised where it meant most to him, in his native Glasgow. In 1923, on 2 October – coincidentally the date on which he was to die years later – he was awarded the Freedom of Glasgow. Tommy was clearly moved by what he called 'the crowning distinction', especially when describing Glasgow as 'the home of my dear parents and a home which I shared with them as long as they lived'. He still carried silver-mounted photographs of them with him whenever he travelled, and when he returned to his private compart-ment on the night train leaving Glasgow that same day they would have been there waiting for him.

For the most part, however, his 1920s days continued to be filled with business. He would drive from Southgate to City Road in London, a journey of some 45 minutes, usually arriving before 10 a.m. and not returning until 9 p.m. If he wanted to dot every 'i' and cross every 't' he had to be there. However, because of his failure to recog-nise the changing marketplace, because he lacked adaptive capacity and because didn't ask the advice of or fully trust his managers, the busi-ness, which had over-extended itself, began to decline.

As the market values of the principal commodities held by the com-pany continued to fall between 1921 and 1924, further new stores were opened. For the year ending 31 March 1923 profits held up, at £337,056. A final dividend of 12.5 per cent was paid. The dividend was reduced to 10 per cent the following year on profits of £292,244. At the twenty-seventh annual general meeting, on Monday, 13 July 1925 at the usual venue of Winchester House in Old Broad Street, Tommy had to admit that 'results . . . had fallen considerably short of expectations'. No dividend was paid on profits of just £142,712 for the year.

By the time 'a most exhaustive enquiry' was launched by Tommy and the directors into the now calamitous state of the business in 1926, the General Strike in Britain, led by the coal miners, had crippled the country. Lipton's profits for the previous year now stood at £25,596. Tommy's own position was no longer tenable. His judgement in the postwar years had been wanting and his blinkered dogged adherence to the same company formula had precluded the benefits of new strategic partnerships or mergers. Quite simply, too, the financial position of the company had been greatly weakened through the payment of dividends in the first half of the 1920s. As Sir John Ferguson, the man who succeeded Tommy as chairman, later noted, instead of paying dividends the company should have been using the money to manage the increase the costs of its machinery and its freehold and leasehold properties.

In 1927 Tommy was effectively removed from office and given the meaningless title of 'life president'. He watched from the sidelines as Lipton's Ltd was taken over by Van den Bergh. Tommy himself was bought out for £750,000. Of course, he was always welcome to visit City Road but by now the excellent relations with his employees that had been such a key factor in his success had all but evaporated. As pressure had mounted in the 1920s he had become even less tolerant and more authoritarian, more suspicious of the motives of managers. In short, he had long since missed the moment when he could have announced his departure and have his staff begging him to stay. It was a sad and ignominious end to an extraordinary fifty-six year run. As for the shops themselves, the 'bad management' referred to by Roy Moxham can be traced to this period, leading to the eventual disappearance of Lipton's in Britain's high streets. Moxham observes, 'In other countries it remained a successful wholesaler, so that now Lipton's name is famous for tea almost everywhere except in the land of his birth.' Though this has changed more recently, it remains true that Lipton is not widely known or acknowledged as one of the great entrepreneurs in Scotland.

The concrete beneath the two heavy green iron gates is cracked. Though no longer used as an entrance from Chase Side to Osidge and Shamrock House, the Sir Thomas Lipton Memorial Home for Nurses, the gates are maintained and the shamrocks and the intertwined letters TJL are still visible. In Southgate, this outpost of the Piccadilly Line between Arnos Grove and Cockfosters, it is still not widely known that these gates on the anonymous tree-lined residential rows of Chase Side hide five acres of garden and several buildings. Secondary among these is Shamrock House, a care home constructed in 1962 that has almost outlived its usefulness and accommodates only four residents. It is joined by a short path to a four-storey Grade II listed Georgian building of light brick that is, simply, Osidge. Mounted above its porch the circular blue heritage plaque reads, 'Sir Thomas Lipton 1850–1931, philanthropist, grocer and yachtsman.' Osidge was his home, his retreat, and never more so than in the 1920s.

The house had originally been built by landowner John Kingston some time between 1800 and 1808. On his death it passed to a Thomas Lambert, who in turn left the house to his nephew, Daniel. But in

1834, just two years later, Daniel sold it to Augustus Bosanquet, a man who had married into the Bevan family. The father of his wife, Louisa, was David Bevan, a Quaker, whose family business of Barclay, Bevan, Tritton & Co. was to become the origin of Barclays Bank.

Osidge was to remain in the Bosanquet family until 1883, when the widowed Louisa died. Exactly how Tommy happened upon it ten years later is not clear, but he needed a home close enough to his London base but far enough from the city. He lost no time in signing up for a 21-year tenancy agreement. Indicating both his love for Osidge and his intention never to return to live in Scotland, he renewed the tenancy agreement in 1914 with an additional option to purchase. And this he did, in 1926.

Osidge was then set in 47 acres of its own grounds. Standing on the white-painted, trellised, Canadian pine balustrade that ran the length of the back of the house, Tommy and his guests could survey the expansive lawns where he entertained so many hundreds of his employees in the golden age. Classical Greek and Roman statues populated the wide, open spaces. Almost symmetrical at either end, close to the balustrade, were giant spreading yew trees whose thick branches overshadowed the mansion and also snaked along, inches above the ground. It was one of these that served as Tommy's treehouse.

Sundry Indian carvings, Japanese bronzes, gold brocade curtains, chairs upholstered in red leather, and a sprinkling of silver-framed photographs brought colour to the interior of the house, reflecting a life spent in global travel. Everything was in its place and everyone knew their role. 'Everyone' included the nine gardeners and three Sinhalese servants, Rodrigo, Louis and John, of whom the former was an accomplished musician as well as a model valet and the latter was the chief butler.

If on his own, especially in this twilight of his life, Tommy would entertain himself by leafing again through his dozens of albums of press notices. These gave him especial pleasure because they focused for the most part on his America's Cup endeavours and the lengthy list of famous personages he had encountered and often befriended. No doubt, with these images and articles fresh in his memory he could regale his dinner guests with tales of his illustrious past. By far the most frequent and important among these guests in the 1920s were four Scotsmen: Tom Dewar (Lord Dewar), Andrew Weir (1st Baron Inverforth), Sir Harry Lauder and Willie Blackwood. In Tom Dewar especially, Tommy had found a kindred spirit. Dewar was a man steeped in the artistry of advertising and salesmanship. Undoubtedly one of the finest after-dinner speakers of his day, he was a gifted raconteur of Scottish sporting and business tales, often at his own expense. Together with his more methodical and serious-minded brother John — who devoted much of his life to the city of Perth, first as city treasurer, then as lord provost, and whose civil service was rewarded when he became Baron Forteviot — Tom Dewar capitalised on the success of his father's Perth business as a wine and spirit merchant. With Liptonesque tactics he took London by storm in 1885 at the age of twenty-one through his employment of a real skirling bagpiper at the Brewers' Exhibition. He followed this up with an illuminated bagpiper who, thanks to clever electric circuitry, repeatedly poured himself a glass of Dewar's whisky on the 200-foot-high north side of Shot Tower by Waterloo Bridge.

Like Tommy, Dewar had a global outlook and he travelled the world relentlessly in search of new business. By 1900 the Dewar business was producing more than 1 million gallons of whisky a year. And, like Tommy, Tom was passionate about sport, particularly horse racing, accumulating more than £250,000 in winnings over the years from horses to whose names he humorously attached the prefix abbot: Abbot's Speed, Abbot's Smile, Abbot's Remorse.

What Tea Tom and Whisky Tom, as the press labelled them, especially liked about each other was their reluctance to talk about business. Whisky Tom much preferred tales of his Abbots and his prize-winning pigeons. He considered pigeon-flying the best sport in the world for the working man. He also supported Tommy in the America's Cup and was a frequent guest on *Erin*.

Like Tommy, Tom Dewar was a single man, and one of the running jokes between them was their search for a wife for the other. Their closeness is perhaps best exemplified, however, by the story of Tom Dewar turning up in one of Lipton's stores in Harrogate in Yorkshire and announcing that he was an inspector from Lipton's head office and was instructed to carry out a thorough examination of the premises. Once shown round, he was so impressed with the way the business was being run he announced that each staff member would be given a rise of £1 a week. Tommy Lipton honoured the increase.

Like Lipton, Harry Lauder couldn't sing high enough praise of his friend Tom Dewar. In his autobiography Lauder states, 'It is one of the greatest pleasures of my life that I am on terms of intimate personal friendship with his lordship.' Tommy Lipton had first met Harry in 1903 when Lauder had a number of engagements in London. He and his wife Annie had bought a house in Tooting. Harry acquired a billiard table and often played host to Tommy and also the young Scottish journalist Willie Blackwood.

As he became the first truly international Scottish star and arguably the first British artist to sell more than a million records, Lauder too was on first-name terms with American presidents of the day and other great artists, like Caruso, and had come a long way from the

Lanarkshire coal mines where he had worked for seven years to support his widowed mother and six younger brothers and sisters. Tommy reciprocated Lauder's earlier hospitality many times over at Osidge. Harry, though, was not an easy guest, ordering staff around and being very fussy about the timing and content of his meals. This was not behaviour he just reserved for his stays at Osidge: he was well known for attending smart dinners, having a word with the headwaiter and substituting his main course with a boiled egg – all because of a delicate digestion, he claimed. Just as well then that plain fare was served up at Osidge. Invariably, soup was on the menu, followed by fish or chicken and then rice pudding and some exotic fruit. Tommy loved his rice pudding and hardly a day went by without it.

From 1920 up to 1926 it often seemed as though Lauder, Dewar and Lipton were inseparable, turning up as they did at the same dinners, attending the opening performance of some show or other. When the *Glasgow Daily Record* organised an interview with the great whisky baron, Dewar rang to say that he was bringing Lipton with him. The *Record*'s writer took the view that it was just as well Lauder wasn't in London too or it would have been a very expensive lunch.

Yet, for all their closeness, for all the banter, there is an unspoken sense that Lipton and Lauder were never quite on the same wavelength. They were not nearly as close as the two Toms, and they were arguably drawn together more by their Scottishness, their celebrity and, latterly, their affection for Tom Dewar than by any real affection for each other. Tommy Lipton is not mentioned once in Sir Harry Lauder's autobiography.

That may be due to a simple oversight, or perhaps to the fact that Harry Lauder engaged the services of Willie Blackwood to help him write it. Blackwood, who shaped Tommy's reminiscences into *Leaves from the Lipton Logs*, sat round the dinner table at Osidge on many an occasion and certainly admired Lipton's achievements, but after Tommy's death he did not disguise the fact that he believed Tommy to be incredibly vain, domineering and self-centred. 'He had to occupy the centre of the stage always,' said Blackwood. It was this absence of humility, especially in the presence of close friends, that really irked Blackwood. That, and the fact that Tommy, as Blackwood recorded it, never acknowledged anyone else's help in getting him to where he was.

There is no reason to doubt Blackwood. He knew Tommy well, worked closely with him on his memoirs and observed him in the company of his closest friends behind closed doors. Yet, apart from Tommy's tetchiness and paranoia towards his subordinates in the declining years of Lipton's as an independent business, he kept this egocentricity and vanity hidden from public view. Of course he loved to name drop, take liberties with the truth in many of his stories and paint himself in a positive light, but somehow he carried it off with a charm and joviality and inexhaustible enthusiasm that made people like him, whoever they were.

The latest edition of the *Oxford Dictionary of National Biography* is much kinder to him than Willie Blackwood is, taking note of his importance to America and to Anglo-American relations: 'He is remembered as one of the most successful businessmen of the time and a devotee of the great sport of yachting, whose splendid hospitality, good humour and inability to accept defeat made him virtually an ambassador of goodwill from Great Britain to America.'

The final Scot around the Osidge dining table, Andrew Weir, came from Kirkcaldy in Fife. As a young man he left his work as a cashier in the Bank of Scotland to join a shipping office. From there he gained enough experience to start his own business, designing sailing ships at first and then moving on to steamships. In 1917 Lord Derby, then secretary of state for war, asked him to prepare a report on the organisation of army supplies. So good were the recommendations that after the war Weir was made minister of munitions and given the huge task of terminating war commitments. He became known as 'the man who saved Britain millions'. For these services he was created 1st Baron Inverforth in 1919. Weir was a neighbour of Tommy's in Southgate and what Tommy liked about him was his terrific energy and enthusiasm. He was a born optimist with a great talent for leadership, combined with generosity. Andrew Weir became a close friend and would later be a trustee of the Lipton estate. After leaving government he went on to become a top industrialist as president of Cable & Wireless, and the founder and first chairman of the United Baltic Corporation. Whilst Tom Dewar and Harry Lauder have left no comment of any note on their feelings about Tommy Lipton, Lord Inverforth described him, almost poetically, as 'A very simple man, the most simple man that I have ever met.'

Tommy loved people to love him. The easiest way to make that happen was to tell stories, with humour, without malice, without being too clever, with him as a principal character in them and with an element of truth – just an element. He had one favourite story in particular that he told again and again, particularly during his last visits to the United States. Unlike many of his other stories, however, this one was probably true in most of its detail: 'So far as I know there is only one man in all America who did not view my three attempts to win the America's Cup with what might be termed an unbiased sporting interest. On the arrival of the third *Shamrock* at Tompkinsville in New York Harbour which was always my anchorage point on reaching the American side, this man wrote to me saying that the windows of his house looked out on the anchorage. He was happily married to an Irish woman of the name of Murphy. And that on the occasion of the first *Shamrock*'s arrival opposite their house his wife celebrated the fact by presenting him with a nice baby boy. "Things went on alright for us," proceeded the letter, "until your second *Shamrock* arrived. On that very day my wife rose to the occasion with a baby girl. Now your new *Shamrock* has arrived and the morning she anchored there was another addition to our family. This time another boy."

"'Now, Sir Thomas Lipton, I am not a millionaire. There are over a hundred million people in America and there is no more loyal citizen among them than I am, but I do hope from the bottom of my heart that you win that darned Cup, but if you don't, on no account come back, or I am a busted man.'"

As a postscript to this true story, Tommy became the godfather to the third child of Mr and Mrs Bergner. The boy was called Thomas Lipton Bergner. And, as Tommy later loved to recall, 'When I went to the States in 1919, this boy called on me and told me his mother was very disappointed because I didn't arrive as expected in September 1914 when another baby was born.'

As the Roaring Twenties drew to a close Tommy reflected in the *Atlanta Journal* of December 1929 on the benefits of playing the team game, in business and in sport, and how the two complemented each other. In the former he saw himself as a team player in his application of a corporate responsibility that gave the business enough profit to function well and, at the same time, benefited the customers and communities who depended upon it. He expounded his cherished belief that sportsmanship 'has become a rule of conduct to be carried into all walks of life and all activities. The notion calls for the same behaviour off the field as on it. It requires that the rules be obeyed without question', but 'to live up to the idea frequently demands a deal of self control that is not always easy to exercise'. And after more than half a century in business and having competed four times for sport's oldest international trophy, he also articulates his understanding of the link between business and sport. It is almost a summation of what he was trying to achieve in both arenas, a kind of corporate values statement, and it has not dated: 'Business has gained a lot from the sports code. Credit and goodwill are largely based on this. Men are finding that it is far better to work together, open and above board, than to try for a quick profit and cut a competitor's throat. Success of one makes success for all – team play with money for the goal. Sharp practice may yield a financial return at the moment, but the dishonest and unsportsmanlike actions will keep the offender away from many a future profit.'

9

Enterprise, the fifth challenge, 1930

Whilst Tommy's star had most definitely fallen in Britain after the involuntary separation from his business in 1927 he retained his celebrity status and business influence in the United States. Not surprisingly, then, it was to America that he returned for an extensive tour in 1927 and 1928. Wined and dined from New York to Los Angeles, he thoroughly enjoyed the attention. In response to all press interviewers the answer was yes, he had every intention of challenging for the America's Cup again. He even told several newspapers that he had made provision in his will that the contest should be carried on after his death by his executors if he had not won the cup in his lifetime.

But why had he let almost ten years go by without a challenge? Undoubtedly one principal reason was the acute disappointment of the 1920 challenge. Quite apart from the timing handicap and the professionalism of Charles Adams's crew, Tommy had not made the right decisions with regard to his captain. Though no yachtsman himself, Tommy had been around America's Cup boats long enough to know that *Shamrock IV*, ugly duckling or not, had been fast enough to win and that he had allowed victory to slip from his grasp. Just how badly Tommy felt about *Shamrock IV* is illustrated by a story told by the authoritative America's Cup historian Jacques Taglang. After the 1920 challenge *Shamrock IV* had been taken to the yard of Bob Jacob of City Island. On a business trip to the United States in 1923, a full three years after the event, Tommy was asked by Jacob what to do with it. Tommy replied, 'Break it up, Bob, and burn it in your chimney. I never want to see that boat again.'

Whilst the smashing up of *Shamrock IV* might have finally laid to rest the ghosts that had haunted Tommy for three years, any resurgence of youthful enthusiasm to re-enter the fray was checked by news of a significant development in 1924. A meeting of the leading representatives of the yachting world from both America and Europe was convened in London with the aim of reaching an agreement on yachting rules. From the early 1900s up to this point the Americans had championed the Seawanhaka or Universal Rule, heavily influenced by Nat Herreshoff. This rule meant that length was regulated, and massive overhangs, like those on *Reliance*, or excessive sail area would be penalised. The Europeans on the other hand had favoured the so-called International Rule with its own length and displacement specifications and focus upon construction standards. The issue was one of measurement. Under the Universal Rule yachts were rated in linear feet and given a letter designation up to the letter 'L'. The International Rule, in contrast, proposed a designation in metres for boat classes. The Americans believed that the Europeans were trying to place limits on what was possible in boat design and technology, and that changes in measurement would seriously impede the development of yacht racing in America.

It was not the fact that the challenger had to cross the Atlantic on its own bottom that really irked Tommy, it was the fact that the Americans could always defend with a yacht of such featherweight proportions – almost a prototype. It could skip across the waves at great speed, but its fragile structure could only withstand a limited amount of racing. *Reliance*, for example, was decommissioned little more than four months after its America's Cup triumph in 1903. In the late 1920s it seemed that Tommy's prayers for a change in rules might be about to be answered, so it would have been foolish of him to mount a fresh challenge until some compromise had been reached. In 1927 the North American Yacht Racing Union and the International Yacht Racing Union agreed and decreed that large yachts had to meet Lloyds standards of construction. In effect, defenders as well as challengers in the America's Cup competition would have to be robust. There was still debate, however, over which rating system would be used.

As the deliberations continued through 1928 and into the autumn of 1929 Tommy continued on what, with hindsight, can be looked upon as a farewell tour of America. One minute he was presenting the Lipton Trophy to the Seattle Yacht Club, the next it was the Sir Thomas Lipton Trophy for the Philadelphia Outboard Regatta. Then it was breakfast with Jack Dempsey or lunch with movie mogul Louis B Mayer. Tommy even asked the legendary Mr Mayer whether he could have a shot at acting, to which he got the reply that the company could not afford his salary, though he did get a tour of MGM Studios and a photo opportunity with Victor McLaglen, a star long before his most famous screen roles with John Wayne. Tommy was also the special guest at a party hosted by the actress Marion Davies. On this occasion, in November 1928, he met Charlie Chaplin, Sam Goldwyn, Maurice Chevalier, Bill Haines and columnist Louella Parsons.

That same month, however, there was an engagement in his itinerary that was to put all others in the shade. In his thirty years of American celebrity Tommy had received many certificates, cups, gifts and other accolades, and a more major one was yet to come, but this one event symbolises more than any other the remarkable impact he had on American life. The Hotel Astor in New York was the setting in November 1928 for a dinner sponsored by Columbia University, the New York Chamber of Commerce, the Merchants Association and the Institute of American Meat Packers. The purpose of the dinner was to honour 'Pioneers of American Industry'. As befitted the occasion, it was an extravagant black-tie affair with 1,700 guests. Speeches from the evening were broadcast on the radio, and press from all over America were in attendance. Photographers had a unique opportunity to picture together the men deemed to have shaped the nation. Tommy wasn't just invited, nor did he have to seek out his place. He was given top-table status and was lined up, seated, for a photograph with the giants of America, some of whom he knew very well indeed.

On the left there was Harvey Firestone. Born in Ohio in 1868, he started life as a book-keeper and patent medicine salesman and went on to establish his own Firestone Tyre and Rubber Company, outwitting his competitors with a new cheaper pneumatic tyre design. Next to Firestone was Julius Rosenwald, the clothier who created Sears Roebuck & Co. Though the company was originally a clothing store, Julius had the vision to diversify into every conceivable household and even farmhouse goods, making millions in the process and changing the face of retail in America. He was also an exceptional philanthropist, particularly for African-American education. Then came another Ohio man, whose father had once been a shopkeeper as well as a land speculator. As a boy he had been fascinated by telegraph and obsessed with the electrical experiments of the British scientist Michael Faraday. From printing telegraphs to the discovery of recorded sound, to the first phonograph, to electric lighting, to the foundation of the company that was, and is, one of the most successful ever created, namely General Electric, his remarkable inventive entrepreneurial contribution to American society and the world was immense. His name was Thomas Edison.

Tommy knew Edison, having played host to him on *Erin* before the war, so it was appropriate that Tommy should be sandwiched between him and another good acquaintance, the steel magnate Charles M Schwab. Seated next to Schwab were two men whose names continue to carry instant global recognition: Henry Ford and Walter P Chrysler. Next to Chrysler was another man who transformed America and the modern world, George Eastman. He had invented the first commercially successful roll film in 1884. He coined the name 'Kodak' for the innovative cartridge film and camera that would replace the heavy dry plates. Eastman was, too, an astoundingly generous philanthropist who gave away $100 million of his fortune. The last in the line-up, and seated on the far right of the photograph, was Thomas E Wilson, who made his fame and fortune from meat packing. Like Lipton, most of these names still live on in recognisable brands.

Iced tea was the preferred beverage of a group of men gathered for a special meeting on 16 May 1929, held behind closed doors on a sweltering hot day in the city of New York. George Cormack, the efficient and popular secretary of the New York Yacht Club, addressed the members of the club's America's Cup Committee seated around the table. He read out the contents of a letter dated 3 May from Richard Barbour, Honorary Secretary of the Royal Ulster Yacht Club, issued on behalf of Sir Thomas J Lipton Bart., KCVO. Although technically it was his sixth challenge, Tommy's fifth realistic challenge now lay on the table. Between sips of tea, the committee deliberated and then decided to accept the challenge. The real question was how to defend. For that they agreed that two syndicates would be formed by the New York Yacht Club, each building one yacht for the cup's defence. The club would also encourage defences from other American yacht clubs.

One of these syndicates would be financed by a member of the Cup Committee who was present at that meeting. He had been elected commodore of the club at the age of thirty-seven, in December 1921. A Long Island boy, he had graduated in law with honours from Harvard in 1907 and served in the United States Navy as commander of a patrol boat. This was followed by a commission to serve on the so-called 'sub chasers' out of Queenstown, Ireland, in the First World War. Cool, methodical and supremely well organised on any size of vessel, he had a natural affinity with the sea, an ability always to make the right judgement. When he was twenty-six he won the first Bermuda yacht race in which he sailed. In his sailing career he would win no less than eight Astor Cups and seven King's Cups, these trophies being among the most prized and prestigious in yachting. What is more remarkable, however, is that 'Mike', which is what he preferred to be called, especially by shipmates, eclipsed his own sailing reputation by inventing the modern game of contract bridge. He did so in 1925 whilst he was on a steamer voyage between California and Cuba. In short, Mike was a clever, cultured, thoughtful and very successful man who cared passionately about sailing and the retention of the America's Cup in the hands of the New York Yacht Club. No one, not even the genial and adored Sir Thomas Lipton would take it away. Although different in almost every other aspect, in this single-minded determination to win he was an exact copy of his great grandfather – the Commodore, Cornelius Vanderbilt. Cornelius Vanderbilt was a Staten Island boy, the fourth of nine children, who bought a sailboat on his sixteenth birthday with a $100 loan from his canny mother, Phebe. His purchase was a flat-bottomed periauger, a simple two-masted workboat, and he used it to ferry passengers across the New York Harbour to the Battery, priding himself on his ability to outrun the competing ferryboats. Sometimes he required every ounce of strength from his muscular 6-foot frame, pushing the boat forward by poles when the wind failed. Using the most colourful language, normally reserved for the mouths of seasoned sailors, he became known as the Commodore.

The Commodore's reputation and income grew. Before he reached his fiftieth birthday in 1844 he operated more than a hundred steamships on the east coast and was already a multimillionaire. Ten years later, the Commodore sold his steamships to the Union at the outbreak of the American Civil War and saw his own wealth rise to $40 million. His association with railroads, with which the family name has become synonymous, did not begin until he was sixty-eight years old. He started modestly with the purchase of stock in a poor-performing Harlem Railroad, barely 130 miles long. From there, he outwitted his new rail competitors to purchase other railroads, eventually merging eleven small railroads to form the 4,500-mile New York Central, of which he became president in 1867. By the time of his death in 1877 at the age of eighty-three, Cornelius Vanderbilt had built a fortune of $95 million. As Arthur T Vanderbilt has noted in his tale of the vicissitudes of the Vanderbilt family, this sum was more than was held in the United States Treasury at that time. He points out that in

1877 'a very successful businessman might earn as much as $10,000 a year'.

Mike – or Harold –Vanderbilt was also following in the more recent family footsteps of his own father and his uncle, who had financed cup defenders around the turn of the century. This 1929 Cup Committee, though, took decisions that would have been almost unimaginable to any of Mike Vanderbilt's predecessors. The terms to be put to Sir Thomas included a change of venue: racing would take place off Newport, Rhode Island, where there were better sailing conditions. Boats were to be built under the Universal Rule, built to a rating of either J or K class, chosen by the challenger. The handicapping system of time allowances was to be abolished. The match would be the best of seven races, not five. Tall triangular mainsails would be adopted for the first time. The mast – a single-part mast, and not a mast with a separate topmast – would be called a 'Marconi', so named for the massive aerials used to transmit radio waves by their discoverer. The rig of the 'leg o' mutton' mainsail set upon it would be Bermudan. With the defender also having to adhere to Lloyds construction standards for the first time, racing would be, in theory at least, on an even keel, though in reality the Atlantic crossing still made additional demands on the challenger. Tommy seemed to have his best chance yet to secure the Auld Mug. He accepted the new conditions and chose the J class of yacht with its specified waterline length of between 75 and 87 feet. On the American side the call for other syndicates to provide a possible defender was heeded. In the event, four J class yachts competed for the privilege of defending the America's Cup: *Enterprise*, *Whirlwind*, *Yankee* and *Weetamoe*. Though L Francis Herreshoff had learned a great deal from his father, the legendary Captain Nat, his *Whirlwind* was no match for *Enterprise*, Mike Vanderbilt's entry. *Enterprise* had been designed by

Starling Burgess, whose own father had designed three winning defenders in 1885, 1886 and 1887 respectively, namely *Puritan*, *Mayflower* and *Volunteer*.

And then, suddenly, it was 24 October 1929, and the boom of the 1920s, in which America had powered far ahead of its industrial rivals, came to an abrupt end. Continuing the trend of the day before, shares were sold at a furious pace and within hours thousands of small investors were ruined. Wall Street crashed and the pain was felt right across America as jobs, homes, businesses and possessions were lost and lives were put at risk through starvation.

Against this background, preparations continued apace for the America's Cup. The combined cost of the four boats built – out of which one would be chosen to defend – was $3 million. The syndicates read like a *Who's Who* of American wealth, from Astors to Morgans to Vanderbilts to Whitneys. In hindsight and with 21st-century values, it is difficult to understand why they should have been so insensitive to the suffering around them at this time by investing so much money in what was, effectively, just a yacht race. One cynical answer might be that they were rich and powerful and insulated from the harsh reality of millions of others. Another is that they simply didn't care – they could do what they liked with their money. A more charitable explanation is that they were great patriots, men who championed innovation, who recognised what the America's Cup said about the technology and progress of America and saw that losing the cup at a time of national crisis would plunge the country into even deeper despair.

And if these were the genuine aspirations of the financiers of this defence, they could not have been delivered a better rescue package than *Enterprise*. Knowledgeable yachtsmen of the day could, and did, wax lyrical about her unusual steel frames and bronze plating, her advanced below-deck winches, and even her 67-foot long, 2,380-pound boom, nicknamed Park Avenue because it was so broad. Of her 26-man crew, 17 were stationed permanently below decks, so it is no wonder that *Enterprise* became popularly known by names like 'box of clockwork' or 'robust robot'. The technology was indeed revolutionary for the day, but it was on deck that *Enterprise*'s greatest advantage lay. This was not the twelve-sided super-light duralumin mast that was at least a ton lighter than *Shamrock IV*'s, but the afterguard of *Enterprise*, her core tactical crew, of which Mike Vanderbilt was the head. It was this afterguard – skipper, helmsman, tactician and navigator – of Vanderbilt, Starling Burgess, CF Hazemeyer and light air helmsman, Sherman Hoyt that was to prove formidable in mastering the technology, mobilising the crew and making the right calls.

Tommy didn't know any of this when he selected Charles Nicholson as the designer of *Shamrock V* in 1929. Nicholson had experience of designing a number of other yachts in the 70–80-foot range including *Brynhild*, *Nyria*, *Astra* and *Candida*. Since the disappointment of 1920 he had re-established himself as a proven winner in British waters, especially in 1928 and 1929. Nicholson was, in fact, much more experienced in designing racing winners of 70 feet or more than the new generation of American designers, Messrs Burgess, Crane, Payne and Herreshoff Jnr, who sought to continue the wizardry of Captain Nat.

Fully thirty-one years since his first *Shamrock* rolled down the slipway, Tommy's latest challenger created once more a carnival atmosphere and an air of expectant optimism. The setting this time, on a sunshine-and-showers Monday in April 1930, was the yard at Messrs Camper & Nicholson in Gosport on the south English coast. Gosport's streets were decorated with flags. As the hour of the launch approached, great crowds surged towards the dockside for a better view. The common consent was that Charles Nicholson had done a fine job and that *Shamrock V* was indeed a beautiful vessel. She was constructed of steel, pine, elm, mahogany, spruce and teak, and her wet green hull sparkled in the sunlight. More critical observers remarked upon her high freeboard and lack of sheer.

The vast crowds, the cheers, the dockyard caps in the air, the sirens and hooters, the 200 guests for the extravagant luncheon, the tide of goodwill from the Royal Ulster Yacht Club articulated by Lord and Lady Shaftesbury and the veteran vice commodore, Colonel Sharman Crawford, the pats on the back from the most celebrated British yachtsmen of the day, none of these could disguise the fact, as Major Heckstall Smith who stood on the launch platform that day later remarked, that Tommy Lipton was 'entirely alone – one man, one designer, one boat'. It was not Tommy's or the British way to form a collaborative decision-making syndicate. By contrast, the America's Cup Committee decision had effectively put the defender out to tender and the resulting competition battle-hardened them in competition against other yachts of the same class and displacement. Although *Shamrock V* encountered no rigging or spar problems in her twenty-three trial races in British waters and performed well enough under Captain Heard she was not thoroughly tested by equal opponents.

As always when Tommy challenged, the real victor was the America's Cup itself. He kindled a broader public interest, enhanced the cup's reputation and elevated it to a level of national sportsmanship that had not been seen before. His grace in defeat time and time again won over more than one entire nation. And, sadly for Tommy, a man now into his eighties in 1930, his good grace would be required once more. From the start of the first race against *Enterprise* on 13 September – a

15-mile run to leeward and return – to the end of the fourth race on 18 September, the outcome was never seriously in doubt. *Shamrock V* managed to hold on for a defeat of less than 3 minutes in the first race, but in the second outing two days later, on a 30-mile course of three equal legs, she was totally outclassed, crossing the line more than nine and a half minutes behind *Enterprise*. The misery was unrelenting. Only 48 hours later, in match three, her main halyard broke and she was forced to retire while *Enterprise* coasted home. The rout was completed on 18 September with *Enterprise* retaining the America's Cup with 5 minutes and 44 seconds to spare.

In the American victory the Vanderbilt factor was indisputable, with Mike and his superb afterguard combining seamanship with professionalism and clever use of psychology to devastating effect. Mike Vanderbilt, a perfectionist who left nothing to chance, even worked out mathematically how a helmsman could best position his boat at the starting line just as the starting gun was fired. Every crew member was given a number and a jersey with that number on it. Typically, in his own account of the 1930 campaign, Vanderbilt analysed the reasons for *Enterprise*'s convincing victory. These were: the lighter mast and rigging; 'a more diversified set of headsails'; better use of sail combinations for the conditions encountered; and, as he put it tactfully, the fact that '*Enterprise*'s afterguard had a greater appreciation of the value of tacking to leeward.'

Though *Shamrock V* was lacking in almost every critical department – speed, preparation and onboard expertise and technology, in which she showed no real advance on *Shamrock IV* – *Enterprise* was exceptional. In the 1930 season she broke two course records of which the main one was in the final match against *Shamrock V*. On that September day she sailed 30 miles in 3 hours 10 minutes and

13 seconds at an average speed of 9.45 knots, breaking the America's Cup race record made by *Columbia* in 1901 by 3 minutes and 5 seconds. Mike Vanderbilt's America's Cup glory was just beginning: he would triumph again in 1934 and 1937. As Ian Dear succinctly put it in his America's Cup history account, 'He made the British look, during the three challenges of the 1930s, what they were: talented amateurs.'

The key questions about Tommy Lipton's America's Cup life are not related to how much publicity or revenue it generated for him or his business, although it is beyond doubt that both column inches and a reputation for commercial success mattered to him greatly. And the cup did create enormous publicity – Tommy's collection of press cuttings alone is testimony to this. The collection is dominated by America's Cup stories, and with each volume at least 300 pages long, containing on average five cuttings on a page, there are probably more than 120,000 America's Cup press cuttings alone. As to whether this translated into business success, the profile and presence of Lipton Tea in America certainly expanded in both the pre- and postwar years, and in the prewar years particularly a strong dividend was maintained. Whilst the America's Cup effect was not measured or analysed in any way, Tommy's extraordinary popularity and celebrity in the United States from 1899 onwards could only have been good for business and seems to correlate with expansion. However, the first central question that must be asked is what did Tommy himself think he had achieved in his five challenges, or six even, counting the unrealised 1907 attempt?

Tommy may not have left any diaries or correspondence, but we do know whether he thought it had all been worthwhile by views expressed at the end of his life, particularly those in his May 1929 article for the *Spur*, entitled 'The Joys of Yacht Racing'. Of course, from a cynic's perspective anything Tommy ever said or wrote was styled almost as a sound bite, a press release or an after-dinner speech. However, in this article we see a man, now in his eighties, reflecting on a passion that shaped the second half of his life. By this age and stage he was beyond media spin; he did not need to ingratiate himself with any individual, class or nation, as cynics may perceive him to have been doing throughout his life.

You would be forgiven for thinking that the author of 'The Joys of Yacht Racing' was a boy. It has a *Swallows and Amazons* feel to it. Tommy writes with a simplicity and a dreamy enthusiasm, calling the sea a 'playground of sailors'. He describes how there will be bigger and faster mechanical ships in the future, but these will never detract from the skill and beauty of sailing a racing yacht. Tommy continues, 'It is something more than skimming over the scintillating white-capped sea. It is an adventurous wrestle with primitive nature and the complete enslaving of all her capricious moods.' In fact, he becomes almost lyrical in his enthusiasm for a sport in which he never played a competitive role himself. 'With spinnaker set and bellied, balloon jibs bending the top mast, and mainsail stretching its utmost to catch every breath of wind, a racing yacht resembles a great bird under human control guided by the hand of man.' Though writing a year before Mike Vanderbilt's *Enterprise* crew would take the synchronised performance of yacht and sailors to new levels, Tommy underlines the fact that the best-designed yacht counts for little without the finest sailors to sail her. Never was this truth more starkly apparent than in the *Shamrock IV* and *Resolute* contest of 1920.

He does not discount his disappointment in this and his other three America's Cup losses, but he takes great pride in his haul of other yachting trophies. The mood and content of this article make it obvious that the America's Cup was indeed the pinnacle of his yachting endeavour, on which his hopes and ambitions were pinned. Equally, however, they make it clear that this was not just a cynical exploitation of a sport for fame and glory. In what we would now call his sponsorships around the world and in the unnumbered *Shamrock*'s competitiveness in British waters, he demonstrated an extraordinary commitment to yacht racing and water sports generally over a prolonged period of time.

As far as a sporting legacy goes, to look upon Tommy as the man who failed to win the America's Cup is to see him in too narrow a perspective. What comes across so strongly in his article and in the closing chapters of *Leaves from the Lipton Logs* is his sense of achievement in popularising a sport that he genuinely believed had no rival for sheer excitement and human skill. His own winning contribution was a limitless supply of enthusiasm from deep within his being, together with a seemingly endless reserve of charm and an ability to find the right words in the right accent for every encounter, whether with press or presidents or the man and woman in the street. It is not difficult to picture Tommy enthralling people on his travels with tales of America's Cup excitement when he writes like this: 'From the moment we jockey for position on the starting line and are off at gunfire till the moment of re-crossing the line, winner or loser, either is thrilling so long as the sport has been hotly contested and human endeavour and better judgement on the day has won. It is one breathless thrill.'

By his own account, what he felt he had achieved in his America's Cup challenges was, in a word, joy. Too easy, perhaps, with modern, 21st-century sensibilities to dismiss such an assertion, and to say that where winning, wealth, immortality, acceptance, recognition or even business success are involved they must be the motivating factors. Frankly, we might say it is naive to believe Tommy. However, while it is true that these all meant something to him, the truth is that they were secondary concerns, merely grounding his enthusiasm in reality. They gave an essential justification for his actions, and he could not have sustained his 31-year passion for winning the America's Cup without a genuine enthusiasm. His real achievements, as he saw them, were to fill a void at the heart of his own life, and to infect people the world over with his enthusiasm for sportsmanship, sailing and this most venerable of trophies. He could truthfully say of the America's Cup, 'in the quest of it I have spent some of the happiest hours of my life. Neither money nor time nor trouble have marred my joy. America's Cup hunting has been my principal recreation for over thirty years. It has kept me young, eager and hopeful.' And on yachting as a whole he could hardly contain himself: 'To me it is a great and satisfying sport brimful of memorable adventure, complicated yet simple, modern yet ever primitive where one is called upon to give battle or to tease the waves, to challenge or flirt with the waves and in the conquest of both to gain a joy unspeakable.'

In his poem 'Enthusiasm' Samuel Ullman says that in every being's heart there is a love of wonder, 'a sweet amazement of . . . the undaunted challenge of events, the unfailing childlike appetite for what comes next'. In the central place of each person's heart, he says, there is a wireless station that, throughout life, should be receiving messages 'of hope, cheer, grandeur, courage'. But when the wires go down and 'the central places of your heart are covered with the snows of pessimism and the ice of cynicism then you are grown old indeed'. The wires did not go down for Tommy. He remained positive and optimistic to the end of his life. In his eighties, Tommy could tick almost

every imaginable box on the 'been there, done that' list: business success, celebrity, philanthropy, knighthood, royal connections, failure, war
service. As Ralph Waldo Emerson put it, 'Nothing is achieved without
enthusiasm', and Tommy approached everything with enthusiasm, a
trait that is arguably less bountiful in the cool twenty-first century. And
it is his remarkable achievement, his inspiration and his most relevant
legacy that the wires never went down. He did not succumb to cynicism or bitterness or a win-at-all-costs strategy in the America's Cup
or in business. He proclaimed a gospel of hard work, fun and fair play,
win or lose.

Tommy was not religious – though out of respect for others, and not
forgetting the example of his parents, he would not race on a Sunday,
and he ordered flags to be at half mast when he heard of the death of
Pope Leo XIII. It would certainly be taking it too far too say that sailing brought with it a spiritual dimension for him, but it gave him a
deep purpose beyond himself, as a faith in God might do.

Why did he not win the America's Cup in five actual attempts?
There are of course individual sets of circumstances and obstacles cited
for each challenge. After Tommy's defeat at the hands of the Deacon
and *Resolute*, however, the British media once again trotted out familiar reasons – some might say excuses. First, the conditions of the Deed
of Gift itself whereby a challenger had to sail across the Atlantic were
a serious handicap. Second, the American defenders not only had
nearly a year's notice of the challenger's intentions, they were also able
to construct more than one yacht to meet the challenger and thus 'try
out the best of the bunch'. In contrast, the original Deed of Gift had
required the challenging yacht club to declare the dimensions of its
challenging yacht six months before the contest. The experienced
British yachtsman Major Heckstall Smith, in commending the talents

of Charles Nicholson, for example, noted prophetically, 'He is immensely handicapped, indeed cruelly handicapped, in this trial of scientific yacht architecture, by being confined to one challenger.' Thirdly, the rating of the boats was not unfair per se, but it tended to favour the normal as against the out-of-the-ordinary boat such as *Shamrock IV*. And finally, the weakest argument of all, there were lighter airs off Sandy Hook than around the British Isles. In truth, there is no single reason for Tommy's failure to win. The temptation that must be resisted, however, is to place contemporary sporting values on a bygone era. The opening lines of LP Hartley's novel *The Go-Between* ring true here: 'The past is a foreign country: they do things differently there.' There was technology, yes, but basic and limited in testing compared with the inexhaustible computer simulations of today. There was competitor analysis, or rather sizing up, but nothing like the zoom-lens data-driven culture of modern racing. There were team incentives and team building, but nothing like the focused and self-motivated discipline of today. The Lipton age of America's Cup spanned the Victorian and the Edwardian eras. It resumed in the post-First World War era and reached into the period of the Great Depression. Whilst Tommy played a crucial role in embedding America's Cup values and giving them deep roots in these tumultuous years punctuated by war and social change, it was Mike Vanderbilt's approach to the 1930 America's Cup that so emphatically closed the Lipton age. Though professionalism and meticulous planning were not entirely lacking in the four previous successful defences against Lipton, with Vanderbilt they were more ingrained and had a harder edge. Even if Tommy had lived another ten years and wanted to challenge yet again, as he originally thought of doing, he would almost certainly have faced stronger domestic opposition. His age would definitely have worked against him, but

Vanderbilt also clearly exposed the weakness of the British method of challenging for the cup. In short, one man alone could not win the America's Cup, no matter how deep his pockets. Even when the rules were more advantageous to the challenger, as they were in 1930, the Lipton philosophy of 'the best money could buy' had proved inadequate against teamwork, training, clinical organisation, technology and innovation.

The man who challenged America was just that – one man. He delegated, he cajoled, he instructed and he attracted the world's attention, but his selection of the 'best designer' and the 'best skipper' was not enough. In its own way each of Tommy's challenges lacked cohesion, a sense of solidarity between owner, skipper, designer and crew, and flexibility. Tommy made his decisions at the start of the process and stuck to them; time and again, problems with different vital elements of each challenge – trial preparation, technology, handling of sails, leadership on board, racing experience of the crew – betrayed an absence of co-ordination and a failure to adjust strategy.

It is curious, perhaps even inexplicable, that Tommy, who was so admiring of the American attitude, did not learn lessons from the first three challenges. It wasn't the Wizard of Bristol, Captain Nat Herreshoff, who won the America's Cup in 1899, 1901 and 1903, nor for that matter was it Charlie Barr: it was a combination of Herreshoff's design, Oliver Iselin's management, Barr's seamanship and the crew's experience and training. It is possible that initially there was a private or tacitly understood agreement between Lipton and Edward, then Prince of Wales, to banish the memory of the Dunraven episode with a thoroughly honourable British approach. On the other hand, as the cynics would have it, perhaps Tommy was only interested in the publicity for his business, at least for the first two challenges.

Whilst there are only grains of truth in these explanations, it is worth restating here one of the real paradoxes of Lipton's life. On the one hand, he exercised such compassion, a warm plain-spokenness that allied him with his humble origins and put kaisers and presidents alike at their ease. He won public affection for the potent mix of good grace in defeat and his indomitable spirit. On the other, his hard-won achievements – based on his intuition – through thirty years of graft in business made it much harder for him to change his way of doing things. He possessed only two of the four traits necessary for success-ful leadership identified by the modern business writer Warren Bennis in his book *Geeks and Geezers*. He certainly had a 'personal voice' that brought with it authenticity and character, and he was well endowed with 'integrity' too, but he lacked 'adaptive capacity' and he certainly struggled with his 'ability to create shared meaning'. These shortfalls cost him dearly in his own business and in his America's Cup chal-lenges, all five of which were cast in his image.

Some blend of his own enthusiasm, integrity, straightforward nature, at times truly asinine arrogance and the distractions of a full social cal-endar deflected his energy away from his key task of leading his team in a fully focused challenge. He was not wily enough for, nor was he really interested in, any provocative psychological battle to rile his opponents. The man who challenged America loved America and loved the quintessentially British values of sportsmanship and fair play too much. Whatever happened, he was determined that he would not be an embarrassment to his own country. Neither would he offend the American people he loved so much.

Though he ultimately failed, Tommy made an inestimable contribu-tion to the evolution and standing of the America's Cup. He is rightly acknowledged in its Hall of Fame alongside those other great yachting

Scots of his era – Charlie Barr, William Fife III and George Watson. Inevitably and appropriately, the Hall of Fame also recognises the men who played their part in sustaining the New York Yacht Club's remarkable 132-year unbeaten run, the longest winning streak in sporting history; familiar names from the Lipton era and the so-called golden age such as Nat Herreshoff, Oliver Iselin, W Starling Burgess, Sherman Hoyt and Mike Vanderbilt all feature. More recent winners in the Hall of Fame include Australian businessman Alan Bond, whose controversial Ben Lexcen-designed *Australia II* succeeded where Tommy Lipton and so many others failed. Alan Bond had persevered through three previous unsuccessful attempts, with *Southern Cross* in 1974, *Australia* in 1977 and *Australia* again in 1980. He had his revenge in 1983 and all of Australia rejoiced.

Alan Bond, in his autobiography, has noted of the successful 1983 *Australia II* campaign, 'we had reached that position through tenacity and our determination to learn from our three previous campaigns'. In addition, to win, the Australians pushed technology, innovation, team spirit and indeed the America's Cup rules to the limit. When the *Australia II* returned to its home city more than 750,000 people turned out for the street parade. As Alan Bond also reflected, the 'historic win made headlines across the country for weeks'.

Another indomitable spirit, Sir Peter Blake, proved again in 1995 that it was possible for a nation, and a small one at that, to win on its fourth attempt. What made this New Zealand *Black Magic* victory so special was that the entire team beat together as one pulse. They recruited an expert in management studies, Peter Mazany. With his help, mission values were articulated and lived. Trust was built up through adherence to tasks and codes of conduct as well as working within tough budgetary constraints. And through the whole endeavour ran two other vital threads: a deep respect and loyalty to Peter Blake, who was a leader and yachtsman of the first order, and a sense of both privilege and responsibility in representing such a small and proud sailing nation in the global arena. Peter Blake summed up the mood of all New Zealanders: 'Sailing for us is like baseball in America or football in Europe . . . they [the Americans] hadn't taken into consideration the expertise and the enormous will to win that exists in New Zealand as well as the vast amount of experience acquired in all types of competitive sailing over the years.'

Bond and Blake are examples of modern Hall of Fame men who challenged America and savoured the victory that eluded Tommy. Though of a completely different time and culture, their experiences offer a glimpse of how a Lipton triumph might have been received. Not all challengers in modern times have been as fortunate as Alan Bond and Peter Blake, though. Baron Marcel Bich, the French business tycoon of Bic pen and disposable shaving blade fame, made four unsuccessful challenges in the 1970s and early 1980s.

The baron was not able to benefit from the change in the rules that he had persuaded the New York Yacht Club to accept, losing out in a series of races among several challengers. Over time, as Bruno Troublé who sailed with Bich as an America's Cup competitor has pointed out, 'The competition among the challengers slowly became tougher than the one held to select the defender.' Consequently, the New York Yacht Club lost its grip on the cup.

To understand why Sir Thomas Lipton was unsuccessful in his five racing attempts to win the cup, Bruno Troublé recommends a visit to the elegant model room of the New York Yacht Club. There 'you'll understand the [British] designs were wrong . . . In all of this period the British boats were narrow, deep and heavy while the Americans' looked like saucepans.' As for Baron Bich, he could easily have been passing comment on Lipton's fruitless challenges when he remarked to Bruno Troublé and others, 'If you want to win the America's Cup you have to be robbers. You have to come with new ideas. If you are very respectful and use the same tools, same sails, same everything as the Americans, you will never win.'

In his will Tommy bequeathed the gold cup presented to him on behalf of the American people, appreciative of his style, warmth and gracious conduct in the wake of his 1899 defeat, to the New York Yacht Club. Today the cup is proudly displayed by the club at the entrance to its library. Thirty years after the American people's spontaneous gesture of goodwill, Tommy was overwhelmed again by the reaction of the defending nation to him, now vanquished for the fifth time. Nearly three months after *Shamrock V*'s defeat Tommy was back in New York. On the morning of 4 December 1930 a specially convened reception committee of the mayor of New York, accompanied by mounted police, gathered outside Tommy's hotel. By the time Tommy stepped out into the unusually sunny winter-morning light, his escort was ready. The New York streets along which this extraordinary procession wound its way were lined with cheering people – all the way. As Tommy approached New York City Hall the band struck up 'See The Conquering Hero Comes'.

Waving his hat in acknowledgement Tommy was already visibly moved by the display of public affection. Entering the hall he took his place at the top table next to his old friends John Fitzgerald and Baron Collier. The mayor, Jimmy Walker, who knew Tommy well, welcomed him and described him as a 'splendid character, a fascinating personality and probably the greatest sportsman in the history of civilisation'.

In front of him stood a gold cup 18 inches high on a silver base. Beneath a rope border was a delicate design of the America's Cup and around the cup's base was the inscription, 'This symbol of a voluntary outpouring of love, admiration and esteem is presented to the gamest loser in the world of sport.' How anachronistic this extraordinary acknowledgement of sportsmanship and gracefulness in defeat now seems.

Tommy rose to his feet and thanked Mayor Walker for his kind words. He went on, 'I have never had a higher honour paid to me in my life than that bestowed upon me by the people in the form of this most magnificent Loving Cup. For many years I have felt I would be the proudest man in the world if only I could lift the America's Cup. And the effect of your most wonderful kindness is that, although I have lost you make me feel as if I had won. In short, you have turned a loser into a winner in a most remarkable way. But I shall try again, I shall try.' Suddenly Tommy's voice faltered and without another word he didn't so much sit down as fall back into his chair. Whether or not he was choked with emotion or made dizzy by the heat of the room was not clear. At any rate, prompted by the mayor, one of his staff, Hector Fuller, picked up Tommy's notes and rounded off his speech. Fuller also read out the telegrams. The only notable absentee from the occasion was the American humorist Will Rogers, who sent his apologies by telegram with this message for Tommy, 'You think this is a fine Cup. Say, this is nothing compared to the one we are going to give you when you lose next time.'

The band then began to play the American national anthem, and Tommy tried to rise to his feet but was restrained by Mayor Walker. When the first notes of 'God Save the King' sounded, however, Tommy pushed away the restraining hand and stood as erect as he could.

Tommy was also presented with a bound volume of his American admirers' letters.

Thousands more had gathered outside to cheer Tommy as he left. It was one last hurrah, one last face-to-face encounter with the ordinary people of America. That they had paid for a Loving Cup for him, ordinary people the length and breadth of America, in the time of deepest economic gloom and national despair, left him speechless. Within ten days of Will Rogers having made his suggestion of a cup for Sir Thomas paid for by $1 contributions, $16,000 had been received.

In spite of sad news – such as the death of his friend Tom Dewar and the exile of his friends the King and Queen of Spain – that would have given him even more cause to reflect on the end of an era, Tommy continued to plan for the future. His philanthropy continued too. Early in 1931 he donated £10,000 to the poor of Glasgow in memory of his mother. As James Mackay recounts, when it was 'reported to him that the money had been converted into vouchers entitling the poor to food and coal he was so delighted that he promptly donated a further £10,000'.

Another reason to be cheerful was the news, received in May 1931, that the Royal Yacht Squadron had finally granted him membership. *Shamrock V* flew the white ensign of the squadron that summer, and now eligible to compete in the King's Cup she duly sailed to victory. Gracious to the last, Tommy accepted the trophy in Cowes and did not offend his new fellow members with any cynical or sarcastic remarks. However, there are no reports of him setting foot in the clubhouse or attending the awards dinner.

Negotiations did begin with the New York Yacht Club for a sixth challenge and he even had in mind a grand occasion in Glasgow for 1932 to reunite expatriate Scots, but neither of these would come to pass. Tommy had spent some time in 1931 with Willie Blackwood working through the final draft of *Leaves from the Lipton Logs*, ensuring there was a sufficiently nautical slant in all his recollections. He didn't want there to be any focus on his private life, or wistful reminiscences of mistakes made in love or business. The America's Cup was his true past, present and future, what remained of it. Tommy caught a cold when out driving on 22 September 1931 and quickly deteriorated in the following days. On 1 October he was well enough to play billiards but fell unconscious later that night. Tommy Lipton died in his sleep, peacefully and without pain, in his beloved Osidge at 7.15 p.m. on 2 October 1931.

The funeral service in St George's Church on Buchanan Street in Glasgow was conducted by Dr Cameron Reid. Psalm 23, 'The Flowers of the Forest' and 'Abide with Me' were sung. The cortege then passed down Buchanan Street and further on, down Crown Street in the Gorbals where Tommy grew up and on to Caledonia Road. With the sky only feet off the ground, huge crowds, ten deep in places, gathered in the grey drizzling rain waiting for the long procession to pass by. Up above, young and old hung out of every available window to catch a glimpse of the scene. Eight cars were needed to carry the floral tributes alone, the largest of which came from the Royal Ulster Yacht Club and the New York Yacht Club respectively.

The procession finally reached the Southern Necropolis, where Tommy would be laid to rest with his parents Thomas and Frances. The inscription on the gravestone also bore witness to the brief lives of his brothers and sisters: Mary Ann and Frances, who had died in 1844 and 1848; Margaret, whose weak grip on life had been lost in 1878 when she died as a young woman; and his brothers Christopher and John, his hero, who had died so tragically in 1857. Lord Inverforth, his trusted yachting adviser Colonel Duncan Neill, Lord Provost of Glasgow Sir Thomas Kelly and the man who knew him best of all, his secretary John Westwood, together with James Brooks, Colonel Spens, William Love and Henry Ambrose Snelling, carried the coffin to its plot. In spite of the huge crowds en route, only a few close friends and civic representatives were present at the burial.

Tommy was as generous in death as he was in life. The residue of his estate was to be divided up among the hospitals and institutions in Glasgow and the town of Cambuslang as well as London and Middlesex, including Southgate where Osidge was located. Specific bequests included a sum of £100,000 for the City of Glasgow, to be distributed for the aid of poor mothers of the working classes and their children. Osidge was to become a hostel for nurses in memory of his mother. Other small specific bequests were made as gifts for the staff at Osidge. In essence, he left his entire estate of £1 million gross to charity. Lord Inverforth, a trustee and executor of the will, later confirmed that no arrangements were made by Sir Thomas Lipton 'to endow a fund with the object of recapturing the America's Cup. He considered the proposal but was advised that it was impracticable.'

Of the hundreds of tributes made to Tommy from around the world one of the most personal and memorable was made by Rose Kennedy's father, the legendary Honey Fitz, John Fitzgerald, who knew Tommy so well and had stood beside him as he received the Loving Cup in New York only months earlier. 'He almost always demonstrated the finest traits of nobility and manhood of anyone I had ever met. His life was a great example for young men to pattern theirs upon. He was born in poverty and rose to wealth and fame, yet his reputation was made great, not by that but by his humanitarianism, his philanthropy, his charity . . . He never forgot the humble parents from whom he sprang. I have seen him in the company of great dignitaries and of humble people, in the presence of mayors and governors, kings and princes, but he was always the same. He felt at home in all company and made everyone feel at home with him. It was an achievement for a man without an education . . . able to handle himself with such ease among people in all walks of life . . . I have lost a great personal friend and humanity has lost a great man.'

This fine tribute captures the essence of Tommy's impact on everyone he met. But to fully grasp the sense of disappointment felt amongst even his adversaries at sea that he never did win the America's Cup, one need only read Mike Vanderbilt's diary at the conclusion of the 1930 whitewash: 'Our hour of triumph, our hour of victory is all but at hand, but it is so tempered with sadness that it is almost hollow.' Another Tommy, Sir Thomas Sopwith, would take up the British challenge for the America's Cup in 1934. On the inside cover of the souvenir programme for this fifteenth defence of the America's Cup were to be found these words, spread out on a single page:

In Memory of
Sir Thomas Lipton
The Grandest Sportsman of Them All

Select Bibliography

Newspapers and Journals

United Kingdom

Algie's Newsletter
Daily Chronicle
Daily Express
Daily Mail
The Daily Sketch
The Daily Telegraph
Evening Standard
The Field
Financial News
Glasgow Bulletin
Glasgow Daily Record & Mail
Glasgow Evening Times

Glasgow Herald
The Graphic
Harmsworth Magazine
Hertfordshire News
Land and Water
Liverpool Daily Post
Morning Leader
Morning Post
The Observer
The Outlook
New Women
Newcastle Leader

Northern Whig
Pall Mall Gazette
The Scotsman
The Sentinel
The Sportsman
The Spur
The Star

Stock Exchange Gazette
The Sunday Times
The Times
Tit-Bits
Western Mail
Yachting World

United States of America

American Weekly (Chicago edition)
Atlanta Journal
Boston Advertiser
Boston Globe
Boston Herald
Boston Post
Charleston News
Chicago Inter Ocean
Chicago Tribune
Los Angeles Examiner
Los Angeles Herald
Los Angeles Record
Los Angeles Times
Louisville Courier-Journal
Newport Daily News
New York Advertiser
New York Evening Herald
New York Herald Tribune
New York Journal
New York World

New York Evening Telegram
The New York Times
New York Herald
The Philadelphia Inquirer
Philadelphia Telegraph
The Providence Journal
San Francisco Examiner
Syracuse Journal
The Washington Times

Canada

Halifax Echo
Toronto Mail
Evening Telegram (St John's, Newfoundland)

Books, articles and reports

Alexander, Andrew; Benson, John and Shaw, Gareth, 'Action and reaction: competition and the multiple retailer in 1930s Britain', *The International Review of Retail, Distribution and Consumer Research*, Vol. 9 (July 1999)

Andrews, Allen, *The Whisky Barons* (London: Jupiter, 1977)

Aris, Stephen, *The Jews in Business* (London: Jonathan Cape, 1970)

Battiscombe, Georgina, *Queen Alexandra* (London: Constable, 1969)

Bond, Alan, *Bond* (Pymble: HarperCollins Australia, 2003)

Bridges TC and Tiltman, HH, *Kings of Commerce* (Freeport, New York: 1928)

Chernow, Ron, *The House of Morgan* (London: Atlantic, 2003)

Conner, Dennis, *Comeback: My Race for the America's Cup* (London: Bloomsbury, 1987)

—— and Levitt, Michael, *The America's Cup*, (New York: St Martin's Press, 1998)

Crabtree, Reginald, *The Luxury Yacht, from Steam to Diesel* (Newton Abbot: David and Charles, 1973)

Crampsey, Bob, *The King's Grocer: The Life of Sir Thomas Lipton* (Glasgow: Glasgow Libraries, 1995)

De Maulde, Françoise, *Sir Thomas Lipton* (Paris: Gallimard, 1990)

Dear, Ian, *The America's Cup, an Informal History* (London: Stanley Paul, 1980)

Devine, TM, *The Scottish Nation* (London: Penguin, 2006)

Dewey, Admiral George, *The Autobiography of George Dewey, Admiral of the Navy* (London: Constable, 1913)

Ellis, David Maldwyn, *New York: State and City* (Ithaca: Cornell University Press, 1979)

Evans, Harold, *The American Century* (London: Jonathan Cape, 1998)

Herreshoff, Nathanael Greene and Stephens, William Picard, *Their Last Letters 1930–38* (Mystic, Connecticut: Mystic Seaport Museum, 2001)

Herreshoff, L Francis, *Captain Nat Herreshoff: The Wizard of Bristol* (New York: Sheridan House, 1974)

Hickey, John J, *The Life and Times of the Late Sir Thomas J Lipton* (New York: Hickey Publishing, 1932)

Kay, John A, *Foundations of Corporate Success* (Oxford: Oxford University Press, 1993)

Kennedy, Rose, *Times to Remember* (Garden City, New York: Doubleday, 1974)

Lauder, Sir Harry, *Roamin' in the Gloamin'* (London: Hutchinson, 1928)

Lipton Ltd Annual Reports 1898–1924 (held in Companies House, Cardiff)

Mackay, James, *The Man Who Invented Himself: A Life of Sir Thomas Lipton* (Edinburgh: Mainstream, 1998)

McCallum, May Fife, *Fast and Bonnie* (Edinburgh: John Donald, 2002)

McCullough, David G, *Mornings on Horseback* (New York and London: Simon and Schuster, 1981)

Moss, Michael and Turton, Alison, *A Legend of Retailing: House of Fraser* (London: Weidenfeld and Nicholson, 1989)

Moxham, Roy, *Tea: Addiction, Exploitation and Empire* (London: Constable, 2003)

New York Yacht Club, *The History of the New York Yacht Club, Volume 1* (held in the New York Yacht Club library)

Oakley, Charles A, *Our Illustrious Forbears* (Glasgow: Blackie, 1980)

Pastore, Christopher, *Temple to the Wind* (Guilford, Connecticut: Globe Pequot Press, 2005)

Riggs, Doug, *Keelhauled: Unsportsmanlike Conduct and the America's Cup* (London: Stanford Maritime, 1986)

Rousmaniere, John, *America's Cup Book 1851–1983* (London: WW Norton, 1983)

——, *The Luxury Yachts* (Amsterdam: Time-Life Books, 1981)

Royal Historical Society, *A Guide To The Papers of British Cabinet Ministers 1900–1964* (London: Royal Historical Society, 1996)

Sefton, Alan, *Sir Peter Blake: An Amazing Life* (London: Michael Joseph, 2005)

Shaw, Gareth; Alexander, Andrew; Benson, John and Hodson, Deborah, 'The evolving culture of retailer regulation and the failure of the Balfour Bill in interwar Britain', *Environment and Planning A*, Vol. 32 (2000)

Strong, Roy, *The Story of Britain* (London: Hutchinson in association with Julia Macrae, 1996)

Symonds, Matthew, *Softwar: An Intimate Portrait of Larry Ellison and Oracle* (New York and London: Simon and Schuster, 2003)

Thompson, Winfield M and Lawson, Thomas W, *The Lawson History of the America's Cup* (Southampton: Ashford, 1986)

Thorndike Jnr, Joseph J, *The Very Rich: A History of Wealth* (New York: American Heritage Publishing, 1976)

Vanderbilt, Harold S, *On the Wind's Highway* (New York and London: 1939)

——, *Enterprise: The Story of the Defense of the America's Cup in 1930* (New York: Charles Scribner's Sons, 1930)

Vanderbilt, Arthur T, *Fortune's Children: The Fall of the House of Vanderbilt* (New York: Morrow, 1989)

Walker, Martin, *Makers of the American Century* (London: Chatto and Windus, 2000)

Wallace, William, *Harry Lauder in the Limelight* (Lewes: Book Guild, 1988)

Waugh, Alec, *The Lipton Story* (London: Cassell, 1950)

Wilson, AN, *The Victorians* (London: Hutchinson, 2002)

Wyndham-Quin, Windham Thomas, Earl of Dunraven, *Past Times and Pastimes* (London: 1922)

Index

BIRLINN LTD (incorporating John Donald and Polygon) is one of Scotland's leading publishers with over four hundred titles in print. Should you wish to be put on our catalogue mailing list **contact**:

Catalogue Request
Birlinn Ltd
West Newington House
10 Newington Road
Edinburgh EH9 1QS
Scotland, UK

Tel: + 44 (0) 131 668 4371
Fax: + 44 (0) 131 668 4466
e-mail: info@birlinn.co.uk

Postage and packing is free within the UK. For overseas orders, postage and packing (airmail) will be charged at 30% of the total order value.

For more information, or to order online, visit our website at **www.birlinn.co.uk**

Birlinn *Limited*

IMPRINTS: JOHN DONALD · POLYGON